LOST LANES

36 GLORIOUS BIKE RIDES
IN WALES AND THE BORDERS

JACK THURSTON

LOST LANES

CONTENTS

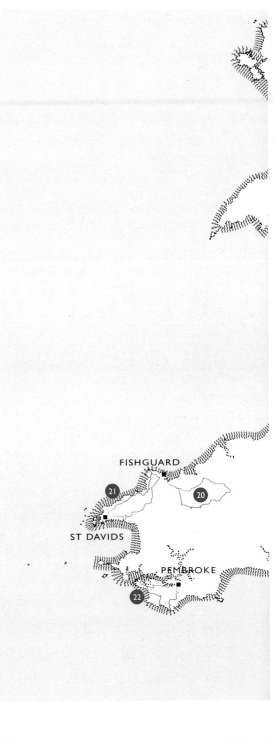

FISHGUARD

21

20

ST DAVIDS

PEMBROKE

22

LLANDUDNO

4

BANGOR

1

LLANRWST

2

DENBIGH

5

CHESTER

23

PORTHMADOG

3

BALA

8

CHIRK

BARMOUTH

7

6

SHREWSBURY

9

MACHYNLLETH

ABERYSTWYTH

BISHOP'S CASTLE

24

25

CHURCH STRETTON

LUDLOW

26

10

RHAYADER

LEOMINSTER

27

12

13

HAY-ON-WYE

HEREFORD

MALVERN

LEDBURY

11

LLANWRTYD WELLS

LLANDOVERY

BRECON

14

28

30

ROSS-ON-WYE

GLOUCESTER

CARMARTHEN

16

ABERGAVENNY

19

LLANELLI

18

17

29

GOWERTON

SWANSEA

BARGOED

PONTYPOOL

15

NEWPORT

CARDIFF

No.	NAME	REGION	NEAREST TRAIN STATIONS	START / END POINTS
1	Heart of Stone	North Wales	Bangor	Bangor
2	River Deep, Mountain High	North Wales	Llanrwst	Llanrwst
3	Harbour to Highlands	North Wales	Porthmadog	Porthmadog/Harlech (train return)
4	The Welsh Riviera	North Wales	Llandudno Junction	Llandudno Junction
5	Hidden Treasure	North Wales		Denbigh
6	An Alpine Adventure	North Wales		Bala
7	Seaside to Sublime	North Wales	Barmouth	Barmouth
8	Over the Top	North Wales	Chirk	Chirk
9	Wool, Wind and Wood	Mid Wales	Machynlleth	Machynlleth
10	The Green Desert	Mid Wales	Llandrindod Wells (17km from start)	Rhayader
11	Llandovery Discovery	Mid Wales	Llandovery	Llandovery
12	Watery Wales	Mid Wales	Llanwrtyd Wells	Llanwrtyd Wells
13	Kilvert's Hills	Mid Wales		Hay-on-Wye
14	Around the Black Hill	South Wales	Abergavenny (9km from route)	Hay-on-Wye
15	Usk Valley Ramble	South Wales	Newport	Newport
16	Three Peaks	South Wales	Abergavenny	Abergavenny
17	Iron Mountain	South Wales	Pontypool, Abergavenny	Pontypool
18	Welcome to the Valleys	South Wales	Bargoed, Rhymney	Bargoed
19	Seaside Seduction	South Wales	Gowerton, Llanelli, Kidwelly	Gowerton/Kidwelly (train return)
20	Only the Stones Remain	West Wales	Fishguard & Goodwick	Fishguard
21	Celtic Coast	West Wales	Fishguard & Goodwick (3km from route)	St Davids
22	Cliff and Castle	West Wales	Pembroke	Pembroke
23	Castles and Cobbles	Borders	Chester	Chester
24	Rock of Ages	Borders	Church Stretton	Church Stretton
25	Blue Remembered Hills	Borders	Craven Arms (13km)	Bishop's Castle
26	Mortimer Country	Borders	Ludlow	Ludlow
27	Wood from the Trees	Borders	Leominster	Leominster
28	Red Planet	Borders	Hereford (16km from route)	Ross-on-Wye
29	In Ruins	Borders	Chepstow	Chepstow
30	Daffodil Dreaming	Borders	Gloucester	Gloucester

MILES	KM	ASCENT(m)	TERRAIN	GRADE
22	35	629	Mixture of lanes, surfaced and unsurfaced tracks	Easy
21	33	501	Lanes	Moderate
24	39	860	Lanes	Challenging
17	27	467	Lanes and a sandy cycle track	Easy
21	34	598	Lanes and an optional 2 mile unsurfaced path	Easy
34	54	1144	Lanes	Challenging
27	43	868	Lanes and a gravel cycle track	Moderate
43	69	1338	Lanes, a long, unsurfaced mountain track ,canal towpath	Very Challenging
34	54	933	Lanes	Challenging
22	35	737	Lanes, optional unsurfaced cycle tracks	Moderate
28	44	797	Lanes	Moderate
18	29	485	Lanes	Easy
26	41	1087	Lanes	Challenging
35	56	1018	Lanes	Challenging
39	62	701	Lanes, short section of surfaced cycle path	Moderate
38	61	1336	Lanes	Challenging
31	50	715	Cycle tracks, canal towpath and lanes	Challenging
26	41	805	Lanes and some gravel mountain roads	Challenging
22	35	120	Surfaced cycle track, some unsurfaced paths, lanes	Easy
39	63	1082	Lanes	Challenging
41	66	901	Lanes	Challenging
31	50	598	Lanes plus a 3 mile section on a gravel path	Moderate
42	67	567	Lanes and two short cobbled sections	Moderate
27	43	920	Lanes and a short section of gravel track	Challenging
24	39	654	Lanes, two short off-road sections, can be muddy after rain	Easy
37	59	888	Lanes	Moderate
46	73	631	Lanes	Moderate
43	68	1013	Lanes	Challenging
29	47	898	Lanes	Moderate
38	61	540	Lanes, short off road section on cycle path	Moderate

IN SEARCH OF

LOST LANES

——

On Easter Monday 1885 Arthur Williams rode a bicycle from his family's farm at the top of the the Amman Valley all the way down to the bustling port city of Swansea. Williams was riding a bike he'd built himself, the first modern, chain-driven bicycle to be built in Wales. The locals who lined the route had never seen anything like it. Williams may have been a bizarre sight on the quiet rural lanes of south Wales, but the coastal roads of north Wales were already established routes for pioneering cycle tourists who rode from Liverpool, Manchester and other industrial towns in search of fresh air and adventure, lush green valleys and mist-clad mountains. They were drawn by the dramatic landscapes that have shaped and defined, contained and protected, blessed and cursed Wales and its borderlands. And those same landscapes continue to delight cyclists today.

When I moved to the Black Mountains of south-east Wales, a big part of the appeal, apart from the romance of returning to the country where I was born, was all the good cycling to be had here. I'd got a taste from many happy holidays in Wales and had already explored much of the country and its borders on summer cycle-camping trips. After a life in central London the thought of simply riding out of my front gate and into the Brecon Beacons National Park was almost too good to be true.

Of Wales's 21,000 miles of roads, a full 60 per cent are narrow, unclassified rural roads. Hiding behind the traffic engineer's dry definition of a lost lane is infinite variety. I've followed lost lanes across heather-clad moorlands, down deep dark gorges, through sand dunes, over salt marshes, along windy cliff tops and over pan-flat floodplains.

I've ridden beneath smooth, towering beech trees and beside gnarled old hedgerows, past shimmering bluebell woods and sun-drenched wildflower meadows. I've watched the seasons come and go, witnessed the searing summer sun, the fire of autumn, the first snows of winter and that most special moment of the year, usually sometime in mid-April, when the russet, khaki and pewter of winter are – almost overnight – replaced by dazzling shades of bright green, and the hedgerow fireworks begin for another year with the first pearlescent fizz of blackthorn blossom.

The old joke goes that if you flattened Wales out it would be bigger than England, and it's true that Wales is considerably hillier that its larger neighbour. Distance is measured in horizontal miles but also in ups and downs. As most of the population of Wales lives in the few flat bits, the simplest way to discover Wales's lost lanes is to follow the road uphill. Mountain roads, whether twisting their way through the vast emptiness of the Cambrians or rising high above densely-packed mining valleys, make for breathtaking bike rides (in both senses). Less obvious on the map, but a joy to discover, are the old ridge roads with panoramic views across vast expanses of rolling countryside. These were the roads travelled by drovers heading east to markets in England with herds of stocky Welsh Blacks and huge flocks of sheep. Clues to identify drove roads are still there: narrow lanes with unusually wide grazing verges; occasional stands of Scots pines planted to mark overnight shelter; and, most obvious of all, the remote inns, most long since shut, with names like the Black Ox and the Drovers' Arms.

But it's not all about the hills. There are gentler lost lanes in the lowlands and along the

coast too, from the cliffs of Pembrokeshire and its patchwork interior to the floodplain of the Vale of Clwyd. And perhaps the greatest concentration of lost lanes perfect for cycling are in the rolling borderlands between England and Wales. Frontiers and edges, the places where one thing gives way to another, are always the most interesting. The author of a 1938 tourist guide to the Welsh borders said its landscape blends "opulence with wildness." Like me, he did his research by bike, concluding that "for appreciation of scenery or for topographical study of the country-side, motoring is far too rapid a mode of motion", essentially the same sentiment as Ernest Hemingway's oft-quoted dictum: "It is by riding a bicycle that you learn the contours of a country best, since you have to sweat up the hills and can coast down them".

The lower Wye Valley is where British tourism was invented, the first of Britain's great landscapes to be 'discovered': Wordsworth wrote poems about it and Turner painted it. In 1875, armed with George Borrow's bestselling *Wild Wales*, William Morris explored north Wales by pony and took what he saw as inspiration for his iconic textile designs. Almost a century later, Allen Ginsberg dropped LSD in the Vale of Ewyas and wrote a long, free-form poem about it. But when you set off to ride "over the hills and far away" you're not just following in the footsteps of the Victorian Romantics and the back-to-the-landers of the late 60s and early 70s, you're joining a trail that goes much further back.

Neolithic nomads, Bronze Age traders and Iron Age warriors all left their marks on the land with tall standing stones, huge burial mounds and spectacular hill forts. The Romans built their roads and camps and founded cities like Carmarthen, Chester and Gloucester. The wandering Celtic monks of the Age of Saints travelled by land and by sea and carried little with them but the word of God. Their lives find a more recent echo in the charismatic, peripatetic preachers of the nonconformist revivals. The roads, lanes and trackways of Wales and the borders have been trodden by invading armies and by migrant workers heading to the mines, quarries, factories and forges. Most of all they have been travelled by ordinary people making ordinary journeys, from farmstead to market, to church and to chapel.

By far best way to see Wales and the Borders is to travel at the speed of the land. By riding a bicycle, you'll be following in the tyre tracks of Edward Elgar, who rode his fixed wheel machine around the Malvern Hills and Herefordshire, composing music as he went. You'll be descending lanes of the Wye Valley where George Bernard Shaw once crashed his bike into Bertrand Russell, the pair landing in a dishevelled heap. If the going gets tough you might sense the shadow of Wayfarer and the pass stormers of the 1920s and 30s, leaning into the wind on the long, hard push along the rough mountain tracks of the Berwyns. You might spot the gap in a hedgerow and the flattened grass where Dorothy Hartley, the great historian of British food and rural life, nestled down for the night, pulling a Welsh blanket tight around her. You might catch a glimpse of the teenage Bruce Chatwin, out of the saddle, cresting the Gospel Pass. You might hear the whirr and click and the panting breaths of the riders in the 1984 Milk Race as they struggled up the Devil's Staircase. And you might even see Welsh cycling greats of today, the likes of Geraint Thomas and Becky James, flashing past in a blur of colour while out training. But if you close your eyes and listen very carefully, you can definitely hear the whoops of joy as the young Arthur Williams zooms down to Swansea Bay.

Jack Thurston, *Abergavenny, 2015*

MAPS AND NAVIGATION

MAPS AND ELEVATION PROFILES

The maps and elevation profiles in the book are all drawn to the same scales. This should aid comparison between routes, in terms of distance and hills. The maps are at a scale of just under 1:100,000. Therefore 1 cm on the map is about 1 km on the road and 1 inch is about 1.5 miles. On the elevation profiles 1 cm is about 150 metres of climbing and 1 inch is about 1,250 feet.

LEAVE THE BOOK AT HOME

This is a heavy book, and the last thing anyone would want to do is carry it around for a day's cycling. That's why all the information needed to ride the routes is available on the Lost Lanes website. At the end of each ride text is a web page address from where you can view and print more detailed maps, download a route sheet or a digital track for navigating with a GPS device or smartphone app.

BEFORE YOU GO

A VIEW FROM THE CLOUDS

—

Consider a single raindrop falling from a cloud floating high above Wales. There are plenty to choose from: Wales gets twice as much rain as England, though less than both Scotland and Ireland. A lucky raindrop might land right on the summit of Snowdon, Wales's highest peak. It would enjoy an exciting 1,085m vertical descent before it reached the sea. Snowdon is a popular choice among raindrops: Crib Goch, the knife-edged arête on Snowdon's northern shoulder, is the wettest spot in Britain.

If the raindrop is blown off course it might land instead on the ragged, boulder-strewn ridge of the Rhinogs, a dozen miles to the south. The Rhinogs, together with the dark giant of Cadair Idris a little further south, are part what geologists call the Harlech Dome. This is Wales's oldest mountain range, and raindrops have been falling here for longer than anywhere else, though their journey to the sea is a short one, just a few miles down the hill into Cardigan Bay.

By contrast, a raindrop that lands in the boggy summit plateau of Pumlumon, just a few miles from the geographical centre of Wales, is in for a much longer ride. For here, in the heart of the Cambrian Mountains, are the sources of two of the great rivers of Britain: the Severn and the Wye. Wales and the Borders – the area covered in this book – enjoys the watery embrace of two river: the Severn, flowing south, and the Dee, flowing north.

If Wales is a land of mountains, then the Borders is a land of rivers, and not just the Severn, the Dee and the Wye. Ceiriog, Tanat, Onny, Clun, Teme, Lugg, Arrow, Honddu and Usk : names that, like the rivers they identify, flow through the long and sometimes troubled history of the Welsh

Marches. March means 'border' or 'boundary' and for centuries after 1066 the Marches were not really England but the semi-independent fiefdoms of Anglo-Norman warlords, a buffer zone to keep the Welsh princes in check. The independent spirit of the border counties – Cheshire, Shropshire and Herefordshire – continues to this day and riding across from Wales into the Borders, the difference is immediate – fine half-timbered buildings, large rambling granges, grandiose churches and huge tithe barns. These are the symbols of the medieval wealth of the area, for the most part a wool economy built on the back of huge flocks of sheep. Today it can cost a farmer more to shear a sheep than its wool is worth and sheep are farmed not for their wool but for the tender meat of their young and, what's more, they have moved uphill to take the place of the small, stout black cattle that once defined the Welsh uplands. Thus even the most apparently eternal rural occupations are subject to the changes wrought by market forces and new technologies, as a hill farmer riding a quad bike will happily admit.

Other raindrops will fall on other ranges: on the Hiraethog east of Snowdonia, on the Brecon Beacons and the Black Mountains in the south, on the Preselis in the west, and to the east, the dark Clwydians, the bare Kerry hills and the labyrinth of the Radnorshire uplands. To the east are the long, humpback ridges of the Shropshire Hills: English waves forever about to break on the Welsh shore. But spare a thought for the raindrop that falls in the upper reaches of the Elan, the Vyrnwy, or any of the many Welsh rivers held back by dams. Raindrops that land there have to wait in the kind of purgatory that is the stillness of an upland reservoir.

Brecon Beacons

Though they've become popular tourist destinations and I'm as partial to a flat road, an impressive dam and a shimmering sunset as anyone, I can't help siding with the poet R. S. Thomas, the grumpy old man of 20th century Wales, who wrote of his sadness and anger at what had been lost beneath the rising tide. Thomas saw the reservoirs – built to supply water to English towns and cities – as colonial acts, symbolic of how England was drowning Welsh culture and consigning the Welsh language to a grave that the Welsh people had themselves dug for it. On the last point he may yet be wrong.

That Welsh has endured on the doorstep of the most successful language the world has ever seen is a remarkable story of survival and revival. It's a story worth celebrating, whether or not you live in Wales or speak Welsh, simply because Welsh is the oldest British language still in use, dating back to the first Celtic settlers some four thousand years ago. King Arthur and the Knights of the Round Table, those great icons of British legend and folklore, would have spoken Welsh,

or something very much like it. English, which evolved from the Germanic tongues of Arthur's Anglo-Saxon enemies and the Old French of the Norman conquerors, is the new kid on the block.

For the English-speaker, learning Welsh (or Cymraeg, to give the language its own name) is a bewildering prospect. There are few familiar linguistic footholds and plenty of false friends. Words shape shift with unexpected mutations, there are new sounds to master and combinations of letters that are unfamiliar to the eye: some Welsh words appear to be made of nothing but consonants! Yet even the most basic familiarity with a new language brings real pleasure and for the touring cyclist a little Welsh has some very real practical benefits. You won't need it to make yourself understood. These days, everyone who speaks Welsh (currently around 20 per cent of the population of Wales) can also speak English but a little Welsh does help in getting to grips with the matter of Wales, starting with the landscape.

Welsh place names often contain a physical description of the place to which they refer. This may well date back to the time, not so long ago in the grand sweep of human history, when people didn't have easy access to maps. Many Welsh place names help to do the work of maps by giving cues for wayfaring. For example, *mynydd* means mountain and *bach* means little, so if your route takes in the village of Mynydd Bach you're in for bit of climbing. The same's true if you see a signpost for the beautiful border village of Grosmont, though that's an Anglo-Norman toponym and instantly recognisable to anyone with a bit of French. The table opposite lists some of the most common landscape features that crop up in Welsh place names.

Though Welsh identity is expressed in the Welsh language, Welsh culture, Welsh history and even a Welsh state of mind, the kingdoms of medieval Wales never coalesced into a single, unified state. The territory was just too mixed up and too mountainous to be easily centralised, and ultimately this enabled Edward I, who set about bringing Wales firmly under English rule, to divide and conquer. In 1282, the Kingdom of Gwynedd, in the north-west corner of present-day Wales, became the last Welsh kingdom to submit to the English crown. Edward consolidated his conquest with a ring of colossal castles that still stand today, and with wealth from farming and mining and a sea link to Ireland, Gwynedd remained the stronghold of political and economic power in Wales. It is still the heart of *Y Fro Gymraeg* (Welsh-speaking Wales) and Gwynedd may well have retained its supremacy had it not been for the industrial revolution, an era that unleashed the most far-reaching realignment of economics, geography and political power that Wales has ever seen.

In just a few decades, the iron industry turned the small upland hamlet of Merthyr Tydfil into the biggest town in Wales, by a mile. The flood of people from the fields to the furnaces meant that by 1851 Wales had become the first country in the world where more of the population worked in industry than on the land. Visiting the vast ironworks of Merthyr in 1850, Thomas Carlyle was shocked: "It is like a vision of Hell, and will never leave me, that of these poor creatures broiling, all in sweat and dirt, amid their furnaces, pits, and rolling mills." After iron, copper, tin and slate came coal, and high-grade coal from the South Wales valleys was exported around the world, sailing out of the sleepy south coast ports whose rapid growth turned the map of Wales upside down. At its peak in the 1920s, one in ten people in Wales worked in the coal mines. Cardiff grew from a population of 1,870 in 1801 to become the largest town in Wales by 1881, a city in 1905 and the nation's capital in 1955.

Development economists talk about the resource curse – the paradox of plenty – and while Wales's abundant natural resources did create huge wealth for the iron masters and mine owners, the lot of ordinary working people was rarely rosy. Even with much improved conditions in the mid-20th century, it was still hard and dangerous work: "Blood and bone is the price of coal", as the ballad goes. Even so, many of those who worked in the mines speak fondly of the strong camaraderie they found there and mourn the passing of a way of life. But the forge and the mine have made immeasurable contributions to Britain, and not just in coal for the navy and iron for the railways.

Industrial Wales was a hotbed of progressive politics, advancing causes that once seemed dangerously radical: votes for all, the welfare state and the right to join a trade union. The National Health Service, perhaps the most treasured of all British national institutions, was created by Aneurin Bevan, a miner from Tredegar, and based on an earlier system devised by his fellow miners. But as Oscar Wilde might have said, the only thing worse than work is no work, and unemployment has blighted the Valleys since the coal mines and steel works closed. In its own very small way, cycling is contributing to a new Valleys economy, with world-class mountain bike trail centres springing up right across the coalfield. Railway tracks and canals built for long-gone industries are being converted into cycling and walking paths, offering a new way to travel in these unique post-industrial upland landscapes.

Wales and the border counties of England are sometimes regarded as being somehow behind the times. But the times are changing and 'progress' is no longer an end in itself. Take a trip to any of 20 or more small to mid-sized market towns and you'll immediately see how much the rest of Britain has already lost to sprawl and the rise of the clone town. In the towns and villages of Wales and the Borders, children can still enjoy the freedom of the great outdoors, there's a boom in local food, and many people live a more friendly way of life. With the confidence that comes from ever-increasing self-government and a renaissance in cultural life, Wales is forging its own path more than ever before. The raindrops still fall, but there is much sunshine too. There has never been a better time to cross the border and discover a land that is both very old and refreshingly new. If you're lucky enough to live in Wales, your country is on your doorstep, waiting for you.

FURTHER READING

JOHN DAVIES. *A History of Wales* 2007. A single-volume tour de force.

JAN MORRIS: *Wales: Epic Views of a Small Country* 1984, new edition 1998. Beautiful portrait by one of Wales's greatest writers.

SIMON JENKINS: *Wales: Churches, Houses, Castles* 2008. Useful reference when visiting Wales's many historic buildings.

GERALD OF WALES: *The Journey Through Wales and the Description of Wales* Translated by Lewis Thorpe 1978. Lively contemporary account of Wales in the late 12th century.

PETER FINCH: *Real Wales* 2009. Part history, part guidebook by an acute observer of contemporary Wales.

GEORGE BORROW: *Wild Wales* 1862. Entertaining and bestselling Victorian travelogue.

JASPER REES: *Bred of Heaven* 2012. An English Welshman in search of his roots.

AND LISTENING

The best way to learn a new language is to hear it and speak it. The *Say Something in Welsh* podcasts come highly recommended. *www.saysomethingin.com*

A SELECTED WELSH TOPONOMY:

AFON – river
ABER – estuary or confluence of streams
ALLT – hillside, cliff or wood
BETWS - chapel
BACH – little
BRYN – hill
BRON – hill crest
BWLCH – gap or pass
CAE – field, enclosure
CARREG – stone or rock
CEFN – ridge
COED – wood
CWM – valley or dale
DOL – meadow
DYFFRYN – valley
EGLWYS – church
GARTH – promontory
GLAN – river-bank, hillock
HIR – long
LLAN – church, monastery
LLYN – lake
MAWR – big, great
MELIN - mill
MOEL – bare hill
MYNYDD – mountain
NANT – brook or stream
OGOF – cave
PANT – hollow or valley
PEN – head, top; end, edge
PISTYLL – waterfall
PONT – bridge
PWLL – pool
RHOS – moor
TIR – land or territory
TWYN – hillock or knoll
UCHAF – upper, highest
YNYS – island
YSTRAD – valley or river meadow

For more detail, including a help on pronunciation, see the Ordnance Survey's 'Guide to Welsh Origins of Place Names' at *tinyurl.com/oswguide*

BEFORE YOU GO

Practicalities

———

ROUTES AND MAPS

The rides in this book range from less than 30km to more than 70km but most are around the 40km to 60km mark, which for most is a good distance for a leisurely day's ride, or a half-day ride for the more energetic. I've deliberately refrained from adding timings to the rides, as it's better to ride at one's own pace than somebody else's. Much of Wales and the Borders is hilly country, and this will come as a shock to people used to the flatter lands of much of England. I've tried wherever possible to go around hills rather than over them, but the road does often go up. This will have an impact on the time it takes to ride a certain distance and the basic level of fitness required for some of the hillier rides. I've indicated the total amount of climbing on each ride, which should give a clue as to how hilly it is, and the elevation profiles also help. A good rule of thumb is 10 miles per hour (say, 15km/hour) for a leisurely touring cyclist, including short stops for snacks, drinks, checking maps and adjusting clothing. If the hills get too much, there's absolutely no shame in walking. In the very early days of the Tour de France, most riders – including those who won the race – pushed their heavy bikes up the biggest mountains.

The maps in the book are best used in combination with a good paper map, such as the Ordnance Survey's 1:50,000 Landranger series. They are costly but can be borrowed from most public libraries or viewed and printed online from *bing.com/maps* or *gpxeditor.co.uk*.

As well as the little maps in the book, printable route sheets and GPS navigation files for each ride are available online. Each ride has a four-digit code that can be appended to the Lost Lanes website URL, as follows: *thebikeshow.net/CODE*

GPS NAVIGATION

GPS navigation is less good for exploring and improvising than a paper map but it excels when following a route that's been planned in advance. For each ride in the book (except the organised group rides) the web page listed at the end of the ride chapter includes a GPX file for use in a GPS navigation device or smartphone using a map and navigation app such as Viewranger. A great cycle touring resource is the *cycle.travel* website, which very kindly provided the maps in this book. If relying on an electronic device for navigation, pack spare batteries or a charging pack.

TAKE THE TRAIN

I have tried to make the rides accessible by train, but the railway services in Wales and the Borders are by no means comprehensive. 'Two Together' railcards offer big savings as do 'Small Group' tickets for groups of three or more. Breaking a return journey is a good way to get more value from a single fare, and Arriva Trains Wales allows unlimited breaking of an open return journey, including overnight breaks, as long as the ticket is still valid (usually they are valid for one month). Check with other train companies for their rules. Many trains in Wales and the Borders are small, two or three carriage affairs, and there are often only two bicycle spaces. Booking in advance is the best way to secure a stress-free journey and avoid the disappointment of a full train. Some train companies restrict access to certain trains during peak weekday commuting times, when most trains are at their busiest. If the train already has its full complement of bikes then a pleading look and heartfelt gratitude can work wonders. After all, train conductors are only human.

ANY KIND OF BIKE

The rides in this book can be ridden on any bike that's in good mechanical order and the right size for the rider. Low gearing makes climbing hills much easier. A triple chainring and/or at least a 30-tooth rear sprocket is recommended. Tyre choice makes a huge difference to the sensation of riding a bike. Good quality tyres between 28mm and 40mm in diameter are a sensible all-round choice for a fast and comfortable ride. Avoid really knobbly tyres as they slow you down on the roads. A touring bike is an ideal choice: the Dawes Galaxy has always been a good place to start but a new breed of crossover and 'adventure road' bikes is a very promising option for the touring cyclist who wants more of a road-bike feel. These bikes have the lightweight feel of a road bike but with modern disc brakes that perform well in all weathers, nice, wide tyres and all the fittings for racks and mudguards if required.

Wales has a reputation for rain, and the statistics confirm it gets more of the wet stuff than eastern Britain. The compensation is the lush green hills and all the sparkling rivers and lakes. Check the forecast at the Met Office website

(or the app for smart phones) and be prepared to ride accordingly. It's no fun pushing on through a monsoon; better to take cover until the storm passes, as they usually do. Unless it's the middle of a heatwave, mudguards should be considered an essential item: it's one thing being rained on from above, it's quite another having a jet of mucky water sprayed up from below.

PRACTICALITIES

LIGHTS, LOCKS AND LUGGAGE

When riding in the dark, a set of lights is a legal requirement. Good lights are well worth the money, and modern battery-powered LED lights are nothing short of amazing. On dark country lanes, supplementing lights with reflective material is a good idea.

In the countryside, a lock is often unnecessary but can be a good precaution, especially if you plan to leave your bicycle unattended for any length of time. A small cable is enough to deter an opportunist but in cities or large towns, where professional bike thieves may be lurking, it makes sense to pack a heavier, more secure lock. If riding in a group, a single lock can secure several bikes.

Money, a basic tool kit, a snack and a mobile phone can be stuffed into a very small rucksack, bumbag or in the rear pockets of a cycling jersey. Anything heavier is more comfortable if carried on the bicycle itself, in either a handlebar bag, a saddlebag or a pannier.

CLOTHING AND SHOES

Despite of the images of lycra-clad racers presented in magazines and on television, the overwhelming majority of people in the world who ride bikes do so in perfectly ordinary clothing. Of course, there's nothing wrong with indulging a taste for the latest cycling gear and donning a cycling uniform of one kind or another, but the reality is that whatever clothing is comfortable going for a walk in the park will be fine for riding a bike in the country-side for a few hours.

Tight jeans with raised seams can be uncomfortable on longer rides. Padded shorts or underwear provide extra comfort if needed. In heavy rain, thick cotton and denim gets water-logged, won't keep you warm and takes longer to dry than wool and synthetic, technical fibres.

Riding in the rain isn't much fun, but lightweight, breathable waterproof fabrics like Gore-Tex Paclite are wonderful when compared with old-style plastic pac-a-macs. Many cyclists – including weight-conscious racers – still swear by lightweight nylon capes that keep the rain out while allowing air to flow underneath, thus avoiding the 'boil in the bag' syndrome of a fully sealed garment. For night rides and camping trips, a few extra layers are a good idea, as is a warm hat. In cold weather, thick, windproof gloves keep fingers nice and warm.

Cycling-specific shoes are unnecessary for all but the most speed-conscious racers, but if you like them I'm not going to argue. The way I see it, large, flat pedals with good grip mean I can wear almost any type of shoe. People have cycled many miles in sandals, flip flops, espadrilles, loafers, wellington boots, high-heeled sneakers and blue suede shoes.

WHEN THINGS GO WRONG

Compared with running a car, the costs of main-taining a bicycle, even if all the work is done by a bike shop, is tiny. Assuming the bicycle is in generally good mechanical order, the skills and tools necessary to mend a puncture and fix a dropped chain are enough to guarantee self-sufficiency on day rides. A truly worst-case scenario means phoning for a taxi to the nearest train station.

A basic on-the-road repair kit consists of the following:

- Tyre levers, a pump and a couple of spare inner tubes
- A puncture repair kit
- Screwdrivers and allen keys required for removing wheels, adjusting brakes and tightening the rack, mudguard fittings and seat-post clamp
- A few cable ties (zip ties) can come in handy, and a bungee cord is useful for securing bikes on trains

Learning a little about how a bike works not only saves money but comes with a warm glow of self-sufficiency. Some tasks are best left to a professional, but the basics are easily mastered. If there's nobody around to give a hands-on lesson, buy a bike main-tenance book or look online for instructional videos, such as those by Patrick Field of the London School of Cycling available at *madegood.org*.

RIDING SAFE AND SOUND

Riding a safe distance (at least 1.5m/5ft) from the roadside and any parked cars is much safer than hugging the kerb. Making eye contact with other road users helps everyone get along.

On roads, it is cyclists that suffer most from the boorish attitude that 'might makes right', and we should be at pains to preserve the civility of traffic-free paths shared with walkers, skaters and horse-riders. Be aware that other people are out enjoying themselves too and may not be paying full attention. Approach horse riders with caution and a verbal greeting to let the beast know that you're human.

When leading group rides with slower or less experienced cyclists, rather than speed off and leave the group trailing in your wake, aim to ride at a pace that's no faster than the slowest riders can comfortably manage.

CLUBS AND ORGANISATIONS

Membership of the Cyclists' Touring Club (CTC) or your local cycling campaign group not only helps these worthy organisations campaign on behalf of cyclists, it also brings benefits like discounts in bike shops, member magazines and third party insurance and free legal advice in the very unlikely event of a crash. Most CTC local groups have full programmes of free or very nearly free rides, which are a great way of discovering new places and meeting new people, with an experienced ride leader taking care of all the navigation and planning tea and lunch stops.

There's also a strong online community of cyclists. The CTC has a forum brimming with expert touring and technical advice. Yet Another Cycling Forum leans towards the long distance side of things. Both are lively places to look for advice, to find out about rides, routes and events, all leavened by varying degrees of friendly banter.

The National Trust, Cadw and English Heritage maintain hundreds of amazing properties across the country, but entry fees can be high if you're just making a fleeting visit while out for a day's bike ride. If you're the kind of person who enjoys visiting historic buildings and sumptuous gardens, an annual membership makes sense and all funds help contribute to the upkeep of their wonderful properties. Similarly, the RSPB, the Wildlife Trusts and Plantlife are member-funded charities that do important work conserving and restoring the natural environment and maintain some superb nature reserves.

Finally, another way to immerse yourself in all things bicycle is to listen to The Bike Show, the long-running cycling podcast that I present (*thebikeshow.net*).

BEST FOR

WILD CAMPING

—

Many of the routes in this book could be used as the basis for a short overnight trip with a small tent or bivvy bag. They're best on a long summer evening when there's plenty of time to ride for a few hours, find a remote and beautiful spot and enjoy a simple camp dinner before settling down to a night under the stars, safe in the knowledge that you'll be returning to 'civilisation' the next morning. There's no need for all the stressful preparation and packing for a longer trip. If you forget something, it's no big deal. The worst that can happen is a bad night's sleep.

Rather than cook an elaborate camp dinner, I tend to fill a Thermos flask with something hot and hearty, and perhaps cook up some couscous on a lightweight camping stove; packing a loaf of bread means the stove can be left behind altogether. Perhaps the biggest challenge on an overnight trip is carrying enough water, though in upland Wales you can usually find a clean stream (pack a portable filter if you want to be doubly safe). Two to three litres of water per person allows for drinking plenty while riding, some for cooking in the evening and enough for tea or coffee in the morning. If you do run dry, most pubs will be happy to refill your bottles.

Since moving to Wales I've slept out all over, from a cliff top on the north coast of Anglesey to the top of Garway Hill in the borders, from the vast emptiness of the Cambrian Mountains to the banks of the River Wye and the nooks and crannies of my local hills, the Black Mountains. There's nothing more relaxing than sitting in camp, well fed, relaxing and chatting by candlelight, feeling the cool evening breeze and watching the night sky as owls hoot in the woods and sheep bleat in the valley below. The cares of real life are left far behind. Then again, maybe this is real life and the office is the illusion?

DO IT YOURSELF

Finding a good place for an overnight camping trip is easier with a little preparation. It's worth looking at the Ordnance Survey's 1:25,000 (Explorer) maps to get an idea of promising locations (they're available for free online at *bing. com/maps*). The best spots are on open land or in woods, out of sight of any dwellings, preferably with access from a bridleway or footpath. It's worth taking a little time on day rides to scout out a potential camping spot and make a note of the location for a future trip. If you are camping near a footpath or bridleway, or on the outskirts of a town or village, it's prudent to camp a little way away, out of sight of early morning dog-walkers.

A tent adds weight and can make you more conspicuous, but it gives a sense of security and more protection from the elements and flying insects. Sleeping in a hammock or under a tarp is an interesting alternative to a tent or a bivvy bag. It comes down to a matter of taste: some find hammocks uncomfortable, others dislike the confinement of a tent.

Wild camping is not legal in England and Wales. Either ask for permission from the landowner or take the pragmatic view that as long as you're unseen and leave no evidence of ever having been there, the landowner is unlikely ever to know, or to care, that you've spent the night. Having said that, in the wildest, most remote places that are best for wild camping it's very difficult to find out who the landowner actually is. It's often easier to ask for forgiveness after the act than to seek permission before. Be sure not to disturb any livestock or trample any

crops. Don't light fires without permission, and leave no trace of having been there. Better still, leave the site in a better state than you found it by collecting any litter left by other visitors.

The following rides in this book are particularly well suited for adapting into a wild camping trip.

THE GREEN DESERT (RIDE No. 10)

Army types call it MAMBA country (miles and miles of bugger all) and it's easy to disappear into the Cambrian Mountains and find a place to pitch a tent or unfurl a bivvy bag. Somewhere along the banks of the Elan, a couple of miles west of Pont Elan, would make for a perfect spot for a wild night under the stars. There's little tree cover, so check the weather forecast to avoid being caught out in a storm.

ONLY THE STONES REMAIN (RIDE No. 20)

There's plenty of open country in the Preseli Hills, and finding a flat spot might be the biggest challenge, but it's quite possible with a bit of careful study of the contours and the bridleways that lead off the lanes into the hills. One option is to leave the bikes locked up at the car park just west of Crymych and walk half a mile up to the summit ridge at Foel Drygarn for a bivvy night among the sacred stones.

RED PLANET (RIDE No. 28)

Garway Hill, a bit past the halfway point in this ride, is a great place for a summer bivvy. Watch the sun rise over the colourful patchwork of fields and the distinctive forms of May Hill in the east and the Black Mountains in the west. There's a roofless brick shelter on the summit, once part of a Royal Air Force tracking station, if things get too windy. Alternatively, head to the banks of the River Wye and enjoy a revitalising dip in the morning sun.

ROCK OF AGES (RIDE No. 24)

The Long Mynd is not a place to camp out in a storm; it can get pretty wild up there. But in settled weather, it's a great choice for anyone looking to sleep on a hill. The Mynd is one of a series of ridges that make up the Shropshire Hills

and on a misty morning, when the peaks hover above the thick cloud hanging in the valley, it's positively dreamlike.

THREE PEAKS (RIDE No. 16)

The Brecon Beacons National Park is one of only six certified 'dark sky reserves' in Britain, recognised for the outstanding quality of its night sky and the measures taken to reduce light pollution. On this ride, the obvious place to spend a night stargazing is the Grwyne Fechan valley: just continue along where the road runs out. An alternative is Gilwern Hill. In autumn, when the days are warm and the nights are cold, you may wake to the spectacular 'dragon's breath' mist snaking its way up the Usk valley.

CELTIC COAST (RIDE No. 21)

Pembrokeshire is Britain's only coastal national park, and the north coast has plenty of remote, empty beaches and cliff tops that are perfect for a bivvy night. Just be sure to leave no trace.

BEST FOR

GOURMETS

———

"Pot of hare; ditto of trout; pot of prepared shrimps; dish of plain shrimps; tin of sardines; beautiful beef-steak; eggs, muffin; large loaf, and butter, not forgetting capital tea. There's a breakfast for you!". So wrote George Burrow in *Wild Wales*, of his breakfast at a Bala inn in 1854. Food is still at the heart of the appeal of travelling in Wales and the Borders, from grass-fed Hereford beef and salt marsh lamb to rich, creamy cheeses and artisan sourdough, from cockles and laverbread to Welsh cakes and *bara brith*.

A good food culture depends on sustainable farming and top-quality ingredients. Small-scale artisan producers are hard at work perfecting local traditions and unearthing lost dishes. Nobody benefits from this food renaissance more than the touring cyclist, who can eat everything entirely guilt-free. More than that, the cyclist is best-placed to understand what the French call *terroir*: the unique combination of climate, soil, topography and tradition that is the secret of the very best local foods.

THREE PEAKS (RIDE No. 16)

Abergavenny's annual food festival is one of the biggest celebrations of gastronomy in Britain and attracts celebrity chefs and small producers alike. For a weekend in September the festival takes over the whole town. Spend Saturday browsing the stalls and packing a picnic pannier, and on Sunday head for the hills.

MORTIMER COUNTRY (RIDE No. 26)

Ludlow, the lost capital of Wales, is the food capital of the Welsh borders. It has its own brewery, a handful of traditional butchers, bakeries, delis and a constellation of Michelin-starred restaurants.

CELTIC COAST (RIDE No. 21)

People come to Pembrokeshire for the beaches, but they also come to eat well, as the area has led the Welsh revival of local food. It would be a pleasure to munch your way around this ride.

AROUND THE BLACK HILL (RIDE No. 14)

The Bull's Head in Craswall is an eccentric, charming and totally unique former drovers' inn at at the foot of the Black Hill. The emphasis is top-notch seasonal, local food. Check ahead as it's a small, family-run place, and opening times vary throughout the year.

THE WELSH RIVIERA (RIDE No. 4)

A seaside ride means ice cream and fish and chips. Llandudno, the queen of Wales's seaside resorts, doesn't disappoint. If you're into mussels and happy to cook them yourself, head across the Conway Bridge to pick up a bag from the fishermen on Conway quayside.

HARBOUR TO HIGHLANDS (RIDE No. 3)

This ride passes the salt marshes of the Dwyryd estuary, grazed by sheep whose sweet, tender organically-farmed meat is prized by top Parisian chefs. You can buy straight from the source at Davies' butchers in Penrhyndeudraeth. A small shop in Harlech may just make the best ice cream in all of Wales

BEST FOR

WEEKENDS AWAY

———

All the rides in this book can be done in a day, but some of the longer ones or those that are a little harder to get to make for a great weekend trip with an overnight stay. Much of Mid-Wales and the Borders has so far resisted the march of the clone town. There has never been a better range of places to stay, from tiny campsites where you can get back to nature, through camping barns, youth hostels and holiday cottages (*UndertheThatch. co.uk* has a mouthwatering selection) all the way to grand coaching inns, plush B&Bs and exquisite boutique hotels. The internet makes finding a good place to stay a thousand times easier, but I have indicated a few of my own selections below and in the ride listings.

KILVERT'S HILLS / AROUND THE BLACK HILL (RIDES No. 13/14)

Hay-on-Wye, secondhand book capital of the world, is an interesting place for a weekend away, even if you've not come for the town's venerable literary festival or its young upstart festival of philosophy and music. Alex Gooch bakes award-winning bread and there many excellent independent cafés, pubs and restaurants. The town sits on the river Wye between the Radnorshire hills and the Black Mountains. A weekend might not be enough.

USK VALLEY RAMBLE (RIDE No. 15)

This ride starts in Newport, a short train ride from Cardiff or Bristol and less than two hours from London. It makes for an easy weekend away, staying either at the Clytha Arms or, just a little on, at the Angel Hotel in Abergavenny. The are some other *Lost Lanes* rides in the area and the official Four Castles route in the hills east of Abergavenny.

BLUE REMEMBERED HILLS (RIDE No. 25)

Bishop's Castle is a gem of a small market town. The place to stay in town is the Porch House, a creaking old Elizabethan house, carefully restored in a rustic chic style, where cyclists are especially welcome. An alternative is to stay in Clun, a small, peaceful town part way around the route.

CLIFF AND CASTLE (RIDE No. 22)

It's a long way to Pembrokeshire so it's worth staying a while. The Stackpole Inn is a country pub with rooms that's won a heap of awards for its food. Plenty close by: South Broadhaven beach, one of the best in Wales, Stackpole Walled Garden and salty Stackpole Quay.

WOOD FROM THE TREES (RIDE No. 27)

Kington is another pearl of a Border town on the long distance Offa's Dyke walking path and has a good selection of B&B accommodation. Church House is full of Georgian elegance, while arty Lower Way Farm is on the nearby Hergest Ridge. Gastronomes beat a path to stylish Jules in Weobley and the Stagg Inn in Titley, the first British pub to earn a Michelin star.

Hay on Wye

The Porch House, Bishops Castle

BEST FOR

UPS AND DOWNS

———

Freewheeling down a long hill is an almost indescribable pleasure, like being a bird in flight. But there is a catch: what goes down must also go up. And riding a bicycle uphill is, at the very least, an acquired taste. On the flat the bicycle multiplies a modest effort into effortless speed. On a climb, the tables are turned. Suddenly the miracle machine is a deadweight to carry.

Yet there are times when the climb approaches a state of grace. Every rhythm, from beating heart to heaving lungs to pumping legs and spinning pedals, comes together in a single symphony of ascent. That's why it's so addictive. At other times, the best thing to do when faced with a really steep climb is to get off and walk. All the more time to look around and see what's growing in the hedgerows.

Long Mynd

AN ALPINE ADVENTURE (RIDE No. 6)

Though it craftily avoids the worst bits of the Bwlch y Groes, the most terrifying of all Welsh hill climbs, there are still plenty of reasons to get out of the saddle on this ride in the hills south of Bala.

ROCK OF AGES (RIDE No. 24)

The Long Mynd is a climbers' paradise and, though this route avoids the really killer routes up, there's still some climbing to be done and a truly eye-watering descent into Church Stretton at the end. There are plenty of other climbs in the area: just get a map and head for the hills.

The Tyla

WELCOME TO THE VALLEYS (RIDE No. 18)

Up on the broad crests between the industrial valleys of the South Wales coalfield are mountain roads that may date back to much earlier times. This ride takes in both hill and valley, and includes some climbs that are nasty and brutish, but thankfully quite short.

Gospel Pass

Cwm Hirnant

THREE PEAKS (RIDE No. 16)

The big draw of this ride is the Blorenge mountain, one of the regular fixtures in top-level bike racing in Wales. But instead of following the famous route up the Tumble, it takes the lesser-known eastern ascent, known locally as the Tyla. The descent on the other side is a thrilling, brake-squealing run through ancient beech woods.

AROUND THE BLACK HILL (RIDE No. 14)

The Gospel Pass is the highest paved road in Wales and is a scale model of the big mountain climbs of the Alps, with a steep forested section before a pastured plateau and then a final summit push to the top. The descent into the Vale of Ewyas is even more scenic and it's a long, steady climb up the quiet, pretty Olchon valley on the return journey.

OVER THE TOP (RIDE No. 8)

This is the most challenging ride in the book, not just because of the height of the ascent of the Berwyns but because it's up an unsurfaced drovers' track. A memorable experience is guaranteed, even if you are forced to walk. On the return journey, the climb up above Llangollen is steep and short and followed by a blissful mountain traverse.

BEST FOR

HISTORY

———

In Wales and the Borders, history is written into the landscape, all the way back to the neolithic tombs of the Preseli hills. The Romans left plenty of their marks, from forts at Caerleon and Chester to long straight roads across the landscape. The borderlands have the greatest concentration of medieval castles in Britain. Wales and the Marches are rich in ancient churches and monasteries, some of which date from a time when most of England was still pagan. Many are so remote that they escaped the Puritan hammer and are collectively a priceless treasure trove of medieval art. Centuries of hill farming has shaped the land too, from dry stone walls that have been dated back to the Bronze Age to gnarled old coppiced trees that line the ancient green lanes. The mountain setting of South Wales's industrial revolution is just as wild and dramatic.

USK VALLEY RAMBLE (RIDE No. 15)

The Usk Valley is a condensed tour of Welsh history, from Monmouthshire's best Iron Age hill fort and Caerleon's Roman remains, to the tiny church at Bettws Newydd and some magnificent old stone barns. Usk's eccentric, rambling Museum of Rural Life is a gem.

HIDDEN TREASURE (RIDE No. 5)

Denbigh is full of interesting ruins – the hilltop castle, the town walls, a friary and an Elizabethan church, many of them a testament to the violence of medieval life. Just outside the town is the gloriously oddball Cae Dai 50s Museum, a shrine to the post-war period. Further on is Lady Bagot's Drive, an old carriage drive that's been used by cycle tourists since the 1920s, and the Tree of Jesse stained glass window in Llanrhaeadr-yng-Nghirmeirch.

RED PLANET (RIDE No. 28)

This ride is rich in ecclesiastical and military history, which is often actually carved into the dusky pink sandstone that defines the architecture of the area, from the spectacular Romanesque church in Kilpeck to Pembridge Castle. Garway was once a centre for the Knights Templar, and it's always a pleasure to browse Ross-on-Wye's many antique and rare book shops.

IRON MOUNTAIN (RIDE No. 17)

This ride up the Afon Lwyd and around the Blorenge Mountain is a journey into the crucible of the Welsh iron and coal industries. At Blaenavon are the old ironworks and Big Pit, where former miners turned museum guides will take you underground and share their own experiences of a way of life that came to define South Wales.

IN RUINS (RIDE No. 29)

Much visited, much eulogised, the towering ruins of Tintern Abbey never disappoint. But there's a great deal more history in the Lower Wye, from Chepstow's Norman castle to the ironworks that took over the valley after Henry VIII chased out the monks, and the atmospheric ivy-clad ruins of St Mary the Virgin at Tintern and Runston Chapel.

Tintern Abbey

Garway church

Blaenavon Ironworks

Big Pit

BEST FOR

ARTS AND CULTURE

—

The bicycle has cropped up in plenty of great art, from the Italian and Russian futurists of the 1910s to Ai Weiwei's huge installation 'Forever Bicycles'. Why shouldn't art and culture be part of a great bike ride? From a 12th century Romanesque font to a Kyffin Williams landscape, there's plenty for cycling aesthetes to discover in Wales and the Borders. These rides all include an important cultural destination, from a top gallery, to an artisan workshop, to a landscape with strong literary connections.

THE WELSH RIVIERA (RIDE No. 4)

Founded in 1902 by Lady Augusta Mostyn, Llandudno's Oriel Mostyn began life as a gallery devoted to showing art made by women. It's recently undergone a daring £5-million renovation and dropped the prefix 'Oriel'. The original ornate terracotta facade has been retained, but behind it the gallery has been transformed with the addition of some daring, neo-brutalist gallery spaces and a great café.

WOOL, WIND AND WOOD (RIDE No. 9)

Machynlleth is an arty, free-thinking town with several galleries well worth a visit. Chief among them is Wales's Museum of Modern Art, housed in an old tabernacle and expanding into neighbouring buildings. There are new exhibitions each year, and the permanent collection, which emphasises work by artists living or working in Wales, includes work by Augustus John, Kyffin Williams and Stanley Spencer.

CELTIC COAST (RIDE No. 21)

There is nothing quite like Welsh tapestry, and I've a growing collection of the thick woollen blankets with colourful geometric patterns, both old designs and the latest, modern reinterpretations of the style. The Melin Tregwynt at Abermawr is an 18th century working mill where you can see cloth being woven on huge whirring looms. There's a great café and a shop that sells textiles from the mill.

KILVERT'S HILLS (RIDE No. 13)

This ride begins in Hay-on-Wye, where there'll be no trouble finding a copy of Rev. Francis Kilvert's collected diaries. Reading them will add depth and texture to this ride, which is essentially an exploration of the unspoiled hills and valleys of southern Radnorshire that passes many of the rambling cleric's old haunts.

SEASIDE SEDUCTION (RIDE No. 19)

The artistic icing on the cake of Llanelli's recently restored industrial seashore is the trail of sculptures along the Millennium Coastal Path. Everyone's highlight is 'Walking with the Sea Turning with the Sea', a gigantic piece of land art by Richard Harris.

DAFFODIL DREAMING (RIDE No. 30)

The flowering of English poetry in the years immediately before the First World War owes a debt to the small west Gloucestershire village of Dymock. It was here that Robert Frost, Edward Thomas, Rupert Brooke and others lived in a rural idyll and developed a pared-down style that used simple language and took for its subjects ordinary events and people.

AROUND THE BLACK HILL (RIDE No. 14)

From Raymond Williams and Allen Ginsberg to Bruce Chatwin and Owen Sheers, the Black Mountains have been a powerful inspiration for novelists and poets. This ride takes in two of their long valleys and passes the hamlet where artist Eric Gill set up his commune in the 1920s.

Millennium Coastal Park, Llanelli

Mostyn, Llandudno

Melin Tregwynt, Abermawr

BEST FOR

WILD SWIMMING

——

The late Roger Deakin, ecologist, nature writer, campaigner and inveterate wild swimmer compiled a whole new watery vocabulary to describe the simple, timeless activity of immersing yourself in a natural body of water, be it a river, a lake, a stream or the sea. He not only uncovered obscure, rarely used words associated with wild water – dook, loom, winterburna, bumbel – but also described the feeling of water itself, from a languid, meandering river to a furiously frothing mountain stream. Deakin was attuned to the differences in colour, taste, temperature and even texture of the water he swam in and the variety of aquatic life he encountered. He even coined a new word – *endolphins* – for the thrillingly pleasurable, all-encompassing rush of a wild swim.

Perhaps Deakin's greatest contribution to wild swimming is to have debunked the misapprehension that swimming in nature is somehow a hazardous, daredevil pursuit. It can be, if you ignore common sense, but people die in their own baths each year and we don't plaster bathrooms with warning signs and barbed wire.

Wales, with its long coastline, dozens of rivers and countless mountain streams, has more than its fair share of wild swimming spots. Make sure you're not trespassing on private land, be alert to the strength of the tide or the flow of the river and check the depth before jumping in.

AN ALPINE ADVENTURE (RIDE No. 6)

There's a series of waterfall plunge pools in the clear, peaty waters of the Eunant Fawr stream and at the end of the ride there's a chance to take a relaxing dip in the cool, calm waters of Llyn Tegid (Bala Lake), Wales's biggest natural lake.

CELTIC COAST (RIDE No. 21)

Pembrokeshire's beaches are the best in Britain. Choose between the white sand strands of Aber Mawr and Abereiddy, which also boasts the Blue Pool, a turquoise quarry pool. Continue beyond St Davids for a sunset dip at White Sands Bay.

CLIFF AND CASTLE (RIDE No. 22)

First up on this coastal route is West Angle Bay, a sheltered sandy cove between rocky headlands. Further on, South Broad Haven gets breakers perfect for body boarding.

WATERY WALES (RIDE No. 12)

River swimming spots abound on the River Irfon. A couple of miles off the route on the mountain road west of Abergwesyn is Wolf's Leap, a series of pools among smooth, flat boulders. Further downstream the Wash Pool is a wide sun-dappled pool once used by drovers to wash their sheep.

THE WELSH RIVIERA (RIDE No. 4)

Llandudno isn't the wildest swimming spot in the world, but the huge sand and shingle North Shore beach rarely feels overcrowded. Wilder, and even more scenic, is the West Shore beach with its dramatic mountain views.

Abereiddy

Eunant Fawr

River Irfon

Llandudno

Pembrokeshire beaches

BEST FOR

FAMILIES

———

For new cyclists and younger children, sharing even quiet country lanes with motor traffic can be unnerving. Fortunately, thanks to the dogged work of Sustrans, enlightened local councils, forestry agencies and national parks, every year sees more miles of traffic-free cycling to enjoy. Riverside paths, canal towpaths, off-road cycle tracks and bridleways are an enjoyable, safe and confidence-building alternative to roads and lanes.

For children, exploring new places a rewarding day out. Adult learners will find even a modest journey in beautiful surroundings a pleasurable introduction to what bicycle travel can offer. Some of the rides listed below will need to be adapted and shortened, depending on the age and experience of the riders.

HEART OF STONE (RIDE No. 1)

The traffic-free cycle path that was once a railway line for the slate quarries of Bethesda makes light work of the journey into Snowdonia's mountain landscape, with lots of interesting industrial remains to explore along the way. The path is generally well maintained, though there are a couple of sections on road which require a little care if riding with younger children. Beyond the quarries the terrain gets steeper and may be a bit too much for little legs.

SEASIDE TO SUBLIME (RIDE No. 7)

The traffic-free Mawddach Trail is one of the most popular family cycling routes in Wales, and justly so. From the wooden bridge across the mouth of the river to the long, well-maintained gravel track up the estuary, it's guaranteed to delight. With children and novices it's best to return by the trail rather than taking on the hillier return route.

THE GREEN DESERT (RIDE No. 10)

This ride can be adapted to suit children and novices by starting from at the car park at the northern end of the Penygarreg Reservoir and taking the traffic-free path through the woods. Simply turn back when the time's right but beware, the return journey will be uphill. Alternatively start at the visitor centre at Elan Village and head uphill on the lakeshore cycle path, leaving the descent for the way back.

IRON MOUNTAIN (RIDE No. 17)

This ride is almost all traffic free though probably too long for most children to manage in a single day. But there are plenty of sections that work as stand alone out-and-back rides. The best bits are around Blaenavon and on the canal and railway paths that run east and west from Llanfoist, with excellent views of the Black Mountains. The section between Blaenavon and Brynmawr, for many years a 'missing link' in the area has recently been completed as an off-road track, which is most welcome.

SEASIDE SEDUCTION (RIDE No. 19)

The wide, smooth cycle path along the Millennium Coastal Path around Llanelli is perfect for cycling with kids as there's no motor traffic to worry about and plenty to see along the way. The smoothest, most child-friendly section is between Llanelli and Burry Port, stopping to climb to the top of Richard Harris's huge earth sculpture.

BEST FOR

PUBS

—

Somehow I've never really associated Wales with really good pubs. Maybe it's the pub's Anglo-Saxon roots, maybe it's the nonconformist teetotallers who gave us Welsh villages with four chapels but nowhere to stop for a pint. But there are good Welsh pubs to be found if you're ready to do a bit of legwork. Across the border in England the real ale aficionado is spoiled for choice, with old coaching taverns, drovers' inns and parlour pubs especially worth seeking out.

Sadly, rural pubs are going out of business at an alarming rate, others are losing their character with modernisation. But not every country pub has been made over into a fancy 'restaurant with rooms' or turned into a big-screen sports bar with Saturday night karaoke. Beyond the hard work of dedicated publicans what is coming to the rescue is the resurgence in small-scale brewing. Wales and the Borders are blessed with dozens of fantastic microbreweries, from the Purple Moose in Snowdonia to Kingstone Brewery on the Wye at Tintern, Bluestone in Pembrokeshire to the Celt Experience and Otley in the Valleys, and Hobsons and the historic Three Tuns breweries in the Borders. And that's not even to mention any of Herefordshire's tiny artisan producers of cider and perry.

The Sun Inn, Rhewl

ONLY THE STONES REMAIN (RIDE No. 20)

The Dyffryn Arms, or *Bessie's* as it's known locally, is a front room pub of the old style. Bessie, the octogenarian landlady, is still on her feet – just – and will pour your pint of Bass from a jug that stands in the serving hatch. Chairs and church pews line the walls of the small bar with a quarry-tiled floor, and the regulars chat away in Welsh. On the other side of the Preseli ridge is the eccentric and historic Tafarn Sinc, while Fishguard has some great backstreet boozers.

MORTIMER COUNTRY (RIDE No. 26)

The Sun Inn at Leintwardine is one of the last remaining traditional parlour pubs in Britain: a series of small rooms, very much like a home. When Flossie Lane, England's longest-serving landlady, died in 2009, many feared it was the end of the road but the pub has been saved. Further on along the ride is the excellent Apple Tree in Onibury.

BLUE REMEMBERED HILLS (RIDE No. 25)

There's beer in them hills, the Shropshire hills that is. In Clun the White Horse Inn is a small 16th century inn with a brewery out back. At the end of the ride, The Three Tuns in Bishop's Castle turns the tables: it's a historic brewery with a pub attached. You can't go wrong with either, though you may have trouble riding if you linger too long.

The Sun Inn, Leintwardine

Wayfarer's Bar, The West Arms, Llanarmon

USK VALLEY RAMBLE (RIDE No. 15)

The Clytha Arms is my favourite pub in Wales, and the family-run inn has it all: a great selection of local ales and ciders, outstanding home-cooked food, blazing log fires, an elegant verandah that's perfect on sunny days and a friendly crowd of locals. If you can't pull yourself away, there are a few rooms upstairs for overnight stays.

OVER THE TOP (RIDE No. 8)

You may need some Dutch courage for the crossing of the Berwyns on the unsurfaced Wayfarers route, and a celebratory drink afterwards is certainly in order. On the way up the Ceiriog there are a pair of lovely old drover inns in Llanarmon. On the way down the Dee valley The Grouse Inn in Carrog has good food in a picture perfect location overlooking the river, while The Sun in Rhewl is a tiny Grade II listed drovers' inn that serves great beer from the nearby Llangollen brewery.

The Clytha Arms

BEST FOR

NATURAL WONDERS

Anyone who spends any time riding a bike will know that natural wonders are all around us, from the very first tiny, green buds of spring to an oversized, butter-hued hunter's moon rising on a warm autumn evening. But some are less common and worth travelling for. As with anything to do with the rhythms of nature, timing is everything. And luck always plays a part.

DAFFODIL DREAMING (RIDE No. 30)

Head to the golden triangle in west Gloucester-shire anytime between early March and early April to see fields, meadows, woods and roadside verges sparkling with Lent lilies, or daffodils as they're more often known. These are not the large, cultivated varieties but the delicate diminutive trumpets of the native species, *Narcissus pseudonarcissus*.

CELTIC COAST (RIDE No. 21)

Pembrokeshire has the best wild flowers in Wales. The dry, windswept, salt-sprayed limestone landscape is a harsh environment, which is perfect for wild flowers because fast-growing but nutrient-hungry grasses have a much harder time of it. Spring to early summer is the time to go plant-spotting.

USK VALLEY RAMBLE (RIDE No. 15)

The shimmering iridescent display of bluebells atop the iron age hill fort of Coed-y-Bwnydd reaches its peak in May and forms a vast ocean swell on the smooth, concentric ramparts of the fort, with good views across the Usk valley, bursting with hawthorne blossom.

ROCK OF AGES (RIDE No. 24)

Heather is a mystery. Some years are good, others are not and I've never worked out why. But when

it's in full bloom, the vast swathes of bright purple that clothe the humpbacked hills of the Long Mynd, and the buzz of honeybees gathering the nectar, are a late-summer spectacular.

AROUND THE BLACK HILL (RIDE No. 14)

The Vale of Ewyas and the Olchon Valleys are wildflower havens, and the year follows a regular pattern, though the timings vary. It's snowdrops first then primroses, celandine, cowslips, bluebells and stitchwort followed by red campion and the frothy explosion of cow parsley. Eagle-eyed plant spotters will see orchids too, sprouting up in the verges, fields and meadows.

RIVER DEEP, MOUNTAIN HIGH (RIDE No. 2)

Gorges and waterfalls are one of the big draws in the heart of Snowdonia and the Conwy Valley's Fairy Glen and Swallow Falls are among the biggest and most well known. The rivers are at their fullest in the winter and spring, after heavy rainfall, and this just happens to be the time when there are the fewest visitors.

NORTH
WALES

HEART OF STONE

From the coast at Bangor to Snowdonia's mountain crucible, on traffic-free
cycle tracks that once sent Welsh slate off for export around the world

———

People have been quarrying slate from the mountains of Snowdonia for at least two millennia. For much of that time it was the work of a small number of independent quarrymen. They cut, dressed, packed and sold the slate on, paying a small royalty to the owners of the land where they worked. Landowners were slow to take an interest in the potential value of what lay beneath their estates but that all changed when Richard Pennant, a Liverpool merchant whose own wealth derived from sugar and slavery in the Caribbean, married into Snowdonia gentry and decided to run the slate quarry on his land as a commercial business.

This ride begins at Port Penrhyn, the harbour built by the Pennant family to export slate from the Penrhyn quarry further up the valley. The traffic-free Lôn Las Ogwen is a cycling and walking path along a pair of old railway lines built to carry the slate to port. It's a well-surfaced, smooth path that begins in a wooded nature reserve and soon passes under an imposing red brick viaduct that bears the mainline railway between London and Bangor. A little further on, just after passing underneath the A55, the route crosses the Glas-infryn viaduct, offering fine views over the surrounding countryside.

There is a short on-road section on the B4409 between the village of Tregarth and Bethesda until the Lôn Las Ogwen goes off-road once again, passing through the old slate yards and alongside the giant heaps of spoil from the quarry (for every ton of usable slate there were between nine and 30 tons of spoil). By the mid-19th century, demand was booming and new, more efficient methods of quarrying and transportation were developed. The Welsh slate industry grew and grew, reaching peak production of almost half a million tons in 1898 and employing 17,000 men. Wales roofed the world.

At that time the Penrhyn quarry was the largest slate quarry on earth and remained so into the 1950s. The quarry is still the biggest in Britain but employs only around 200 people. There are no direct views into the quarry from the cycle path but it's easy enough to scramble up one of the huge embankments of spoil to take a look through the wire fence at the giant hole, now an eerie lake of turquoise water.

Just as deep as the pit left on the mountainside are the scars left on the local community by the great strike of 1900-03, the longest labour dispute in British history. Tensions had been building over many years and finally spilled over when trade unions were banned from the quarry. Nearly 3,000 workers walked out in protest and Lord Penrhyn responded by locking them out indefinitely. The battle of wills pitted the wealthy, Anglican,

---

START & FINISH: Bangor • DISTANCE: 22 miles/35km • TOTAL ASCENT: 629m
TERRAIN: Mixture of lanes, surfaced and unsurfaced tracks. Easy.

Penrhyn Castle

English-speaking Penrhyn against the poorly paid, Nonconformist, Welsh-speaking quarrymen. Anyone who broke the strike – and their family – was labelled a traitor and the social divisions the strike caused are still felt to this day. In the end, Penrhyn's enormous wealth meant he could hold out longer than the impoverished quarrymen. Many men had already left the area to find work elsewhere and the quarry never fully recovered. The saga ranks among the key formative events in the emergence of working class politics in Wales.

Leaving the huge piles of slate behind, the ride now begins a sensationally scenic section on a five-star lost lane up the Nant Ffrancon valley towards the mighty rock faces of the Glyderau range. For much of the 1940s the artist John Piper lived in the valley and the powerful landscapes inspired some of his best paintings. On the far side of the valley, hewn into the rock, is the A5 and this carries almost all of the traffic through the valley. Built by Thomas Telford as part of the strategic route from London to Holyhead (and onwards to Dublin), in the 1950s and 1960s it was used for the London-Holyhead professional bike race, at 275 miles the longest unpaced one-day road race in Europe.

This part of Snowdonia is the cradle of British mountaineering and, up at the Nant Ffrancon pass, Ogwen Cottage has been a base for generations of climbers, while Tryfan is one of the few British peaks that demands a bit of scrambling to get to the top.

This is a there-and-back route but it's so spectacular that it's worth riding twice, and there is a little detour on the return leg to keep things interesting. Just before Tregarth, the route turns right across the river and over the A5 towards Rachub. From the cemetery an enchanted lost lane guarded by stout oak trees rolls down towards Penrhyn Castle and the sea, eventually rejoining the Lôn Las Ogwen on the outskirts of Bangor.

Download route info at thebikeshow.net/01HS

PUBS & PIT STOPS

Not many café and pub stops on this route apart from just off the route in Bethesda, so a picnic lunch is recommended.

BLUE SKY CAFÉ, Rear of 236 High Street, Bangor LL57 1PA (01248 355444) The locals' choice for good coffee and cake, breakfasts and burgers. Wood-burner in winter.

THE TAP AND SPILE, Garth Road, Bangor LL57 2SW (01248 370835) No frills student pub near the harbour, pub grub in big portions.

DOUGLAS ARMS, Ogwen Terrace, High Street, Bethesdam LL57 3AY (01248 600219) Just off route, a historic, very traditional old coaching inn that hosts an annual garlic contest.

FITZPATRICKS CAFÉ. 9 Ogwen Street, Bethesda LL57 3AY (01248 602416) Just off route, a friendly, bright green café.

OGWEN SNACK BAR, Nant Ffrancon, LL57 3LZ (01248 600683) Mountaineers' tea bar right by the mountain rescue base. Hot drinks and basic snacks.

YHA IDWAL COTTAGE, Nant Ffrancon, LL57 3LZ (08453 719744) Oldest youth hostel in Wales. Rooms, dorms and car-free campsite.

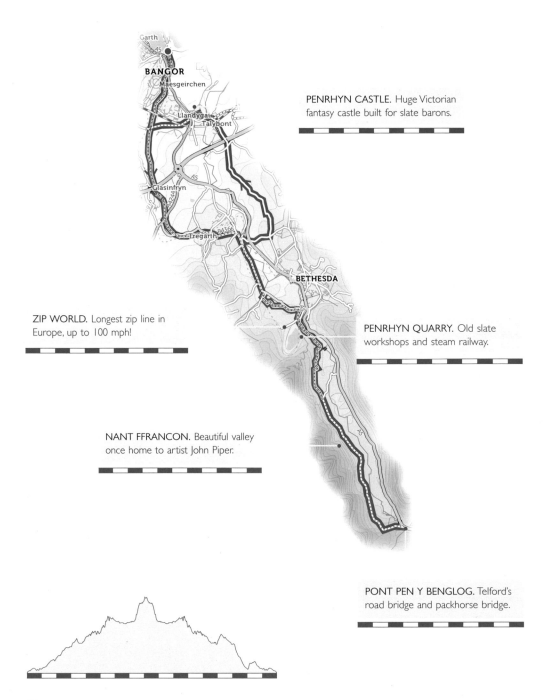

PENRHYN CASTLE. Huge Victorian fantasy castle built for slate barons.

ZIP WORLD. Longest zip line in Europe, up to 100 mph!

PENRHYN QUARRY. Old slate workshops and steam railway.

NANT FFRANCON. Beautiful valley once home to artist John Piper.

PONT PEN Y BENGLOG. Telford's road bridge and packhorse bridge.

Pont Pen y Benglog

No.2

RIVER DEEP, MOUNTAIN HIGH

A journey up the Conwy valley to the ravines and waterfalls of the Fairy Glen
and back via the wild, windswept uplands of Hiraethog

———

Fifth century Britain was a time of flux as many small kingdoms emerged into the power vacuum left by the fall of the Roman Empire. The Kingdom of Gwynedd in the north-west corner of present day Wales was the longest lasting of those states and it preserved Romano-British laws and customs, Celtic Christian beliefs and both the Latin and Brittonic languages longer than anywhere else. Gwynedd soon found itself set against the rising Anglo-Saxon fiefdoms of the east of the country, which practised a pagan religion, spoke Germanic languages and observed their own laws and customs. These two sides – which warred among themselves as much as with each other – were the precursors of Cymru and England (the words 'Wales' and 'Welsh' derive from the Anglo-Saxon word *wælisc* meaning 'foreigner' or 'slave', used at first to describe all the native peoples of the British Isles).

The Kings of Gwynedd ruled a territory rich in minerals with fertile valleys and a long coastline – the Irish Sea has been dubbed the Celtic Mediterranean. Eryri was their mountain stronghold (Snowdonia, by its Anglo-Saxon name). The kingdom maintained its independence until the final, decisive conquest by Edward I in 1282. In the years that followed Gwynedd was invariably the hotbed of resistance to English rule. It remains the stronghold of Welsh (or, if you like, native British) culture, language and traditions.

This ride in the upper Conwy valley takes in the two quintessential landscapes of Snowdonia. First, the famous waterfalls and wooded valleys around Betws-y-Coed that have drawn tourists ever since the Victorian travel writer George Borrow waxed lyrical in his bestselling book Wild Wales. It also explores the wide open expanses of moorland and pasture that, in spite of their scenic charms, few tourists ever visit.

The route starts in Llanrwst, a gutsy market town that hasn't yet succumbed to the tourist hordes that have turned the likes of Betws-y-Coed and Beddgelert into year-round resort towns. Things immediately get off to a good start with the ride over Llanrwst's architectural glory: the 1636 stone bridge, allegedly designed by Inigo Jones, that spans the Conwy in three exquisitely proportioned arches. It's then a gentle spin up the River Conwy to Betws-y-Coed.

After crossing the A5 the route begins a lovely run through the forest, the roar of the rapids on the upper Conwy rarely out of earshot. After a short but unavoidable section on the A470, the lane continues up the river through the secluded 'Fairy Glen' gorge, passing a series of dramatic waterfalls. For a proper look, leave the bikes by the road and walk through the woods towards the sound of rushing water. When crossing the

START & FINISH: Llanrwst • DISTANCE: 21 miles/33km • TOTAL ASCENT: 501m
TERRAIN: Lanes. Moderate

Llanrwst

Machno river look out for a narrow, overgrown bridge. Known as the Roman Bridge, it's actually a 17th century packhorse bridge, although a river crossing here may have Roman origins.

At this point the ride leaves tourist Snowdonia behind and sets out into a glorious, sparsely populated upland landscape of hill farms and open moorland. Much of the land around here is part of the massive Ysbyty estate, which spreads across 8,000 hectares of open moorland and river valleys and encompasses 51 hill farms. Now owned by the National Trust, the estate was once part of the vast landownings of Richard Pennant, the first Baron of Penrhyn. Pennant's fortune was founded on industrial slate quarrying and slave-labour sugar plantations in the Caribbean.

At the heart of the estate is the village of Ysbyty Ifan. A peaceful, attractive, small village today, it was once a staging post on the major pilgrims' route between Chester and Bardsey Island at the tip of the Llŷn peninsula (three pilgrimages to Bardsey were the equivalent of one to Rome). The Knights of St John established a base in the village to provide shelter for pilgrims and gave it a new name that means St John's Hospital. As well as sheltering pilgrims, it's said they provided sanctuary for outlaws too, including the Red Bandits of Mawddwy, a notorious gang of redheaded robbers and rustlers.

From Ysbyty Ifan, the route loops back on the western side of the Conwy valley, through Pentre-foelas and up along the scenic mountain road on the slopes of Moel Seisiog. This road is a dream, with views to the knife-like summit ridge of Moel Siabod and the Snowdon horseshoe beyond. If you're flagging or the light is fading there are plenty of bail-outs on lanes leading back to Llanrwst, but the real temptation on this road is just to ride off into the sunset. The wind farm on the slopes of Moel Maelogen marks the highest point of the ride, and from here it's a glorious descent down to Llanrwst.

Download route info at thebikeshow.net/02RD

PUBS & PIT STOPS

CAFÉ CONTESSA, Ancaster Square, Llanrwst LL26 0LG (01492 640754) Excellent café serving good local food.

ALPINE COFFEE SHOP, Station Approach Betws-y-Coed LL24 0AE (01690 710747) Coffee and cakes right by the railway station.

CAFFI CABAN-Y-PAIR, Holyhead Road Betws-y-Coed LL24 0BN (01690 710505) Funky café serving a good fry-up.

A5 BACON BAR, lay-by on A5 just west of Rhydlanfair (01490 420085) Legendary greasy spoon in a converted caravan.

FOELAS ARMS, Pentrefoelas LL24 0HT (01690 770213) Old coaching inn.

BIKE SHOPS: 1866 Racing, Denbigh Street, Llanrwst LL26 0LL (01492 641028)

Beics Betws, Betws-Y-Coed LL24 0AD (01690 710766) Bike hire available.

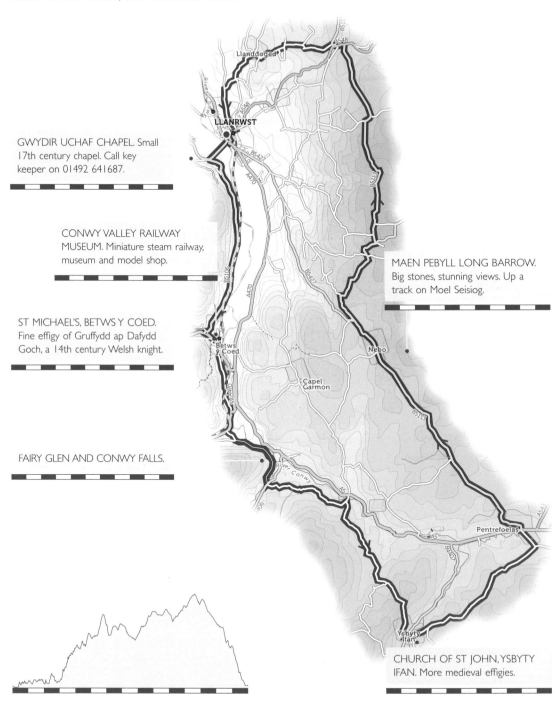

GWYDIR UCHAF CHAPEL. Small
17th century chapel. Call key
keeper on 01492 641687.

CONWY VALLEY RAILWAY
MUSEUM. Miniature steam railway,
museum and model shop.

ST MICHAEL'S, BETWS Y COED.
Fine effigy of Gruffydd ap Dafydd
Goch, a 14th century Welsh knight.

FAIRY GLEN AND CONWY FALLS.

MAEN PEBYLL LONG BARROW.
Big stones, stunning views. Up a
track on Moel Seisiog.

CHURCH OF ST JOHN, YSBYTY
IFAN. More medieval effigies.

Ysbyty Ifan

Moel Siabod and Snowdon

HARBOUR TO HIGHLANDS

In the foothills of the Rhinogs, Snowdonia's most underrated mountain range, discover Bronze Age mystery, medieval history and breathtaking views all around

───

The crowds that flock to Snowdon, Britain's most visited mountain, leave the southern hills that rise above Harlech unvisited, and they are all the better for it. Few have heard of the Rhinogs, yet it's a wild and mesmerising landscape. The proximity to the sea adds another layer of drama to the mountains, especially at day's end when the sun dips towards the long, sea monster silhouette of the Llyn Peninsula, and the glassy waters of the Afon Glaslyn estuary sparkle in the golden light.

The narrow, winding lanes above Harlech see little more than farm traffic but long ago there were important long-distance trackways crossing the Rhinogs. The best preserved is the route from Harlech to Chester via Cwm Bychan. It's shown on maps as the 'Roman Steps', though historians believe it's more likely a medieval packhorse trail. The area is rich in Bronze Age remains, with a concentration of hut circles, standing stones and burial mounds as dense as anywhere in Wales.

This ride begins in Porthmadog, a town that owes its existence to – and takes its name from – William Madocks. He was a well-to-do lawyer, landowner and Member of Parliament. In 1798 he bought a large estate in north Wales, much of it useless sand and tidal marsh, with the intention of transforming it into fertile farmland. To do so he financed the construction of the Cob, a

two-mile-long embankment at the mouth of the Afon Glaslyn, and then drained his land which lay behind it. Diverting the river caused it to scour out a fine new natural harbour: Porthmadog. At first it was used to export slate from the quarries at Blaenau Ffestiniog, carried down the valley on a narrow gauge railway line now run as a tourist attraction. Porthmadog grew into a centre of shipbuilding and is most famous for the Western Ocean Yachts built for the trade in salt cod from Canada, though they carried other cargo as well. Sleek, graceful and quick, the two- and three-masted schooners were among the glories of the golden age of sail.

The traffic-free ride along the Cob offers fine views up the estuary and the route continues by lane into Penrhyndeudraeth and across the brand new bridge, which has recently replaced a rickety old wooden toll bridge. At Llandecwyn the route heads inland and uphill on a short, sharp climb. Even the strongest cyclist will be excused for getting off and walking this one. It's then a long descent through some lush broadleaf woodland before a long, steady and increasingly steep ascent onto the plateau above Harlech.

Working its way east towards the peaks of the Rhinogs, the lane soon descends into the narrow, wooded valley of the Afon Artro (*afon* being

---

START & FINISH: Porthmadog / Harlech (train return) • DISTANCE: 24 miles/39km
TOTAL ASCENT: 860m • TERRAIN: Lanes. Challenging

The Cob, Porthmadog

Welsh for river). It's here that the sheer dampness of Snowdonia becomes overwhelming. There's water trickling along every rill and crevice, the dark rocks are clothed in luxuriously soft, thick moss, and banks of hart's tongue ferns curl and twist like seaweed in an octopus's garden.

The next climb is up Cwm Nantcol and onto the lower slopes of Moelfre. From here there are more great views and a long descent through a fascinating jigsaw puzzle of prehistoric field systems. Fields are demarcated by walls up to six feet thick, built by hand with stones painstakingly cleared from the land. Sheep and cattle graze here now, but the fields would have originally been used to grow crops in the warmer and drier climate of the Bronze Age.

At the bottom of the valley, the village of Dyffryn Ardudwy is home to a cluster of cromlechs (prehistoric burial cairns) that are older than Stonehenge. There's a railway station here, which offers a bail-out option, or else you can continue on more scenic lanes north towards Harlech. Beyond Harlech the roads are flat and fast but can be quite hostile (especially the A496), so it's worth considering hopping on a train for the short journey back to Porthmadog. Otherwise, you could retrace the scenic but decidedly hilly inland route from earlier in the day.

Download route info at thebikeshow.net/03HH

PUBS & PIT STOPS

BIG ROCK CAFÉ, 71 High Street, Porthmadog LL49 9EU (01766 512098) Home baked cakes, picnic provisions.

THE VICTORIA INN, Llanbedr LL45 2LD (01341 241213) Robinsons' pub serving food. B&B available.

HUFENFA'R CASTELL, Harlech LL46 2YH (07810 164547) Right by the castle, possibly the best ice cream in Wales.

LLEW GLAS DELICATESSEN, High Street, Harlech LL46 2YA (01766 781095) Groovy café with top scones and Welsh cheese ploughman's.

MERTHYR FARM, LL46 2TP (01766 780897) Small campsite high above Harlech, huge views.

BIKE SHOP: KK Cycles, 141 High Street, Porthmadog, LL49 9HD (01766 512310)

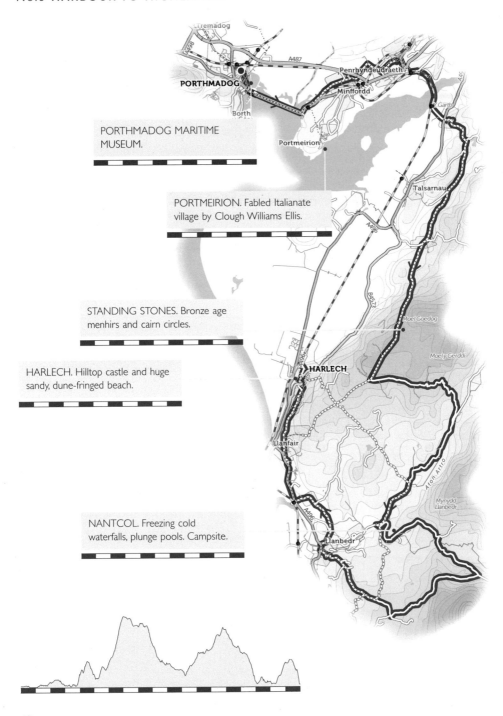

PORTHMADOG MARITIME MUSEUM.

PORTMEIRION. Fabled Italianate village by Clough Williams Ellis.

STANDING STONES. Bronze age menhirs and cairn circles.

HARLECH. Hilltop castle and huge sandy, dune-fringed beach.

NANTCOL. Freezing cold waterfalls, plunge pools. Campsite.

Merthyr Farm Campsite

THE WELSH RIVIERA

A circuit of the Creuddyn peninsula taking in the queen of Wales's seaside resorts
and the dolomite cliffs of the Great Orme

Of the handful of places that describe themselves as the 'Welsh Riviera', the Creuddyn peninsula has the strongest claim. The Llŷn may have better beaches, Tenby might get more sunshine, but half close your eyes and Llandudno's long, gently curving esplanade is Cannes' Promenade de la Croisette, while the cliff-top Marine Drive around the Great Orme headland is the closest Britain gets to the celebrated Corniche des Crêtes. Though not without a few climbs, this is a relatively short route, so it's best to choose a sunny day and take it slowly, stopping off along the way for a dip in the sea, an ice cream on the pier, fish and chips on the beach and maybe a snooze as well. Just remember to pack the suncream.

From Llandudno Junction railway station the route heads inland on Marl Drive, across the A470 and up a long, stiff climb. Do not be alarmed. There are only three climbs on the ride and this is definitely the toughest. On the climb there are views into Snowdonia and up the Conwy valley as well as glimpses of the 64-foot Bodysgallen obelisk. Unlike most obelisks, which date from the 18th and 19th centuries, this is a very modern erection. It was put up in the 1990s by the owner of a hotel and health spa on the site and it took the locals quite by surprise. Snowdonia National Park authority and the local Wildlife Trust backed 700

local people who signed a petition against what they felt was an unnecessary visual intrusion on the skyline. Yet the obelisk still stands.

It's a winding route through a mixture of pasture and woodland, past farmhouses and cottages, many made from the local limestone: light coloured and quite different from the dark granite that's typical elsewhere in North Wales. On the way is the Bryn Pydew nature reserve, a small area of woodland, limestone grassland and disused quarries. It's home to wild orchids, primroses, cowslips and stinking hellebores. Among the insects recorded here are 22 species of butterfly, a staggering 600 species of moth and a small population of glow-worms. At the foot of the hill the route joins National Cycle Route 5 into Penrhyn Bay and then it's a mostly traffic-free route across the Little Orme Head and down through an enclave of grand, Santa Monica-style villas onto Llandudno's long promenade. The promenade is long and wide with room enough for everyone to enjoy – walkers, cyclists, rollerbladers, scooterists and skateboarders.

Llandudno is Wales's largest seaside resort and grew up in the era of the railways that brought visitors from the urban centres of northwest England. The development of the town was masterminded by the Mostyn family, which still owns much of the land

---

START & FINISH: Llandudno Junction • DISTANCE: 17 miles/27km • TOTAL ASCENT: 467m
TERRAIN: Lanes and a sandy cycle track. Easy

Llandudno

Marine Drive

on the peninsula. Carefully planned at the time, the town retains much of what must have made it such an elegant destination: from its ornate cast iron verandahs and balustrades to its gleaming, wedding cake stucco; and from the shimmering Maharajah's palace of a pier to the baroque terracotta facade of the Mostyn gallery. Though it's slipped in places, much of Llandudno's grandeur remains unfaded.

For cyclists, Llandudno's biggest draw is the Marine Drive. I can't think of a more scenic four miles of cycling. It's featured in plenty of rides from regular amateur road races, time trials and cyclosportives to the finish of a stage of the 2014 Tour of Britain. For most of the way around it's one way (anti-clockwise) and a £2.50 toll for cars keeps it relatively quiet. It's a thrilling ride as the road twists and turns around the limestone cliffs rising to 120 metres above sea level. Along the way it passes the old crenellated lighthouse and a small café. Spinning away out at sea are the 160 turbines of Gwynt y Môr wind farm. It's Britain's biggest offshore wind farm and capable of powering 30 per cent of all homes in

Wales. Dedicated hill climbers will take a detour on the summit road to the peak at 207 metres. There's more to see of the Great Orme, too, from neolithic burial sites, a Bronze Age copper mine and the church of St Tudno that gives Llandudno its name, to the rare flora and the herd of wild, white-haired Kashmiri goats that have roamed the headland for more than a century.

Rounding the headland the road descends onto a cycle path between the sand dunes and the beach. This is a storm-prone coastline and the path is often inundated with sand. At worst it means getting off and pushing for ten minutes or so, no great hardship. The cycle track gets better as it rounds the next headland into Deganwy, where it continues up the River Conwy, with views of the dark, rounded walls of Conwy Castle and the mountains of Snowdonia behind. The well-signed cycle route ensures an efficient, mostly traffic-free return to Llandudno Junction station.

Download route info at thebikeshow.net/04WR

PUBS & PIT STOPS

THE QUEEN'S HEAD, Glanwydden LL31 9JP (01492 546570) Upmarket dining pub, rooms available.

FORTE'S, 69 Mostyn Avenue, Llandudno LL30 1AQ (01492 877910) Historic ice-cream parlour.

FISH TRAM CHIPS, 22 - 24 Old Road, Llandudno LL30 2NB (01492 872673) Famously good fish and chips.

TRIBELLS, 10 Lloyd Street, Llandudno LL30 2YA (01492 878296) Take away for fish and chips on the beach.

REST AND BE THANKFUL CAFÉ, Marine Drive, Llandudno LL30 2XD (01492 870004) Café at the highest point of the Marine Drive climb.

THE LIGHTHOUSE B&B, Marine Drive, Llandudno LL30 2XD (01492 876819) Chintzy, but an unbeatable location in an actual lighthouse on the Great Orme.

WEST SHORE BEACH CAFÉ, Dale Road, Llandudno LL30 2BG (01492 872958) Beachfront café with outside seating.

ENOCH'S FISH AND CHIPS. 46 Conwy Road, Llandudno Junction LL31 9DU (01492 581145) More excellent fish and chips, right by Llandudno Junction station.

BIKE SHOP: West End Cycles, Conway Road, Llandudno Junction LL31 9BA (01492 593811)

MARINE DRIVE. The most spectacular four mile road in Wales.

MOSTYN. Recently revamped contemporary art gallery and café.

LLANDUDNO BAY. Big sand and shingle beach.

WEST SHORE BEACH. Kite-surfers' paradise.

CONWY MUSSELS. Fresh mussels from the quayside.

West Shore Beach

Conwy Castle

HIDDEN TREASURE

South of the ancient fortress town of Denbigh into some classic,
off-the-beaten-track cycle touring country

———

The town of Denbigh stands in the Vale of Clwyd like an aged street-fighter: battered and bruised after a lifetime of hard knocks but somehow still on its feet. Built on a strategic hilltop in a long, wide and fertile valley, there has been some kind of fortification here for more than 1,000 years. Armed insurrections after Edward I's conquest of Wales in 1282 saw the town and castle pass back and forth between Welsh princes and the English crown. In 1400, during the Glyndŵr uprising, the town was attacked once more. During the Wars of the Roses it was a Yorkist bastion and the Lancastrians laid it to waste. In Tudor times it rose again to become one of Wales's four regional capitals along with Brecon, Caernarfon and Carmarthen. During the Civil War Denbigh Castle was one of the final Royalist strongholds to surrender to Cromwell's forces. They began the work of dismantling the fortifications and after the restoration of Charles II the castle was simply left to decay.

As well as guarding the Vale of Clwyd, Denbigh stands sentry at the eastern approach to the Hiraethog hills and Snowdonia. *Hiraeth* is a Welsh word for which there is no adequate English translation. It's homesickness tinged with grief or sadness, a mixture of longing, yearning, nostalgia and wistfulness for a bygone Wales. Some say it's a uniquely Welsh sentiment though speakers of Portuguese and Galician come close with *saudade*. Hiraethog, therefore, means something along the lines of 'place of great longing', and the upland plateau and its surrounding foothills are hidden treasures of the Welsh countryside.

This ride takes in its quiet eastern edge, several pretty villages and plenty of rolling countryside that has delighted cycle tourists for more than a century. Throughout there are dramatic views of the Vale of Clwyd itself, all the way north to the off-shore wind farms in the Irish Sea, as well as views east to the brooding hills of the Clwydian Range.

From the ramparts of Denbigh Castle it's a smart descent on the B4501 and over the Afon Ystrad. The route then follows the course of the Ystrad upstream to Nantglyn. This village once had a forge, a pub, a mill, a post office, a shop and school – all now gone. It boasted several churches and chapels and in the churchyard of one of them, the church of St James, stands a sacred yew. The ancient tree contains a stone staircase and a small platform built to be used as a pulpit by preachers including, it's said, John Wesley, co-founder of the Methodist Church.

From Nantglyn the road heads uphill to the village of Saron and along a terrific ridge road

---

START & FINISH: Denbigh • DISTANCE: 21 miles/34km • TOTAL ASCENT: 598m • TERRAIN: Lanes. Easy

Denbigh Castle

with some breathtaking views. It's then a brake-squealing descent to Cyffylliog a little village that sits in a hidden valley of utterly unspoiled countryside. From Cyffylliog the route follows the valley downstream and, for the three-mile section between Bontuchel and Rhewl, there's a choice to be made: either stay on the lane and climb up on the southern side of the valley, or cross over the river and turn right off-road onto Lady Bagot's Drive, a glorious old Edwardian carriage drive along the limestone gorge.

The Bagots were once the local gentry and the drive was built on the course of a railway line that was never completed. Though soft under wheel at times, the drive is perfectly passable on a road bike except after heavy winter rains, when it might be just a bit too muddy. It's been a popular route among touring cyclists for a century. Writing around 1930, Liverpool based cycling journalist Winifred Williams described the gorge as a "fairy land" and vouched that "to see this place in spring or early summer, especially in morning sunshine, is sheer enchantment". It has changed little since her time.

From Rhewl it's a pan-flat couple of miles along the floodplain between the two forks of the River Clwyd to the village and Welsh pronunciation challenge of Llanrhaeadr-yng-Nghinmeirch. An essential stop here is the church of St Dyfnog. The stained glass Tree of Jesse window is one of the greatest surviving works of medieval art in all of Wales, and the carved hammer-beamed roof is none too shabby either. Denbigh is just a few miles further on down the road.

Download route info at thebikeshow.net/05HT

PUBS & PIT STOPS

THE RED LION, Cyffylliog LL15 2DN (01824 710351) Village pub, food served evenings and weekend lunchtimes.

DROVERS ARMS, Ruthin Road, Rhewl LL15 2UD (01824 703163) Friendly pub on a main road, food served.

KINGS HEAD, Llanrhaeadr LL16 4NL (01745 890278) Village pub with restaurant and B&B.

GUILDHALL TAVERN, Hall Square, Denbigh LL16 3NU (01745 816533) Swanky hotel and restaurant in a former coaching inn.

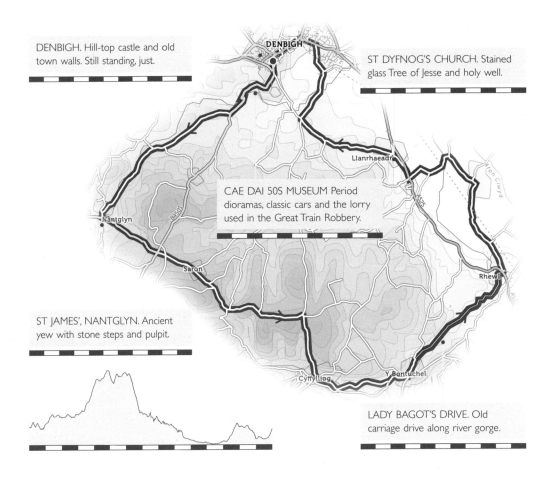

DENBIGH. Hill-top castle and old town walls. Still standing, just.

ST DYFNOG'S CHURCH. Stained glass Tree of Jesse and holy well.

CAE DAI 50S MUSEUM Period dioramas, classic cars and the lorry used in the Great Train Robbery.

ST JAMES', NANTGLYN. Ancient yew with stone steps and pulpit.

LADY BAGOT'S DRIVE. Old carriage drive along river gorge.

St Dyfnog's Church

Cae Dai 50s Museum

No.6

AN ALPINE ADVENTURE

Lakes, mountains, pine forests and upland pastures make for a challenging ride in the big hills around Bala

———

Each July, cycling fans around the world watch the Tour de France unfold on a spectacular stage featuring fairytale castles, vast fields of sunflowers and the azure waters of the Mediterranean. Yet the real drama of the world's biggest annual sporting event only begins when the race hits the high mountains. Clear, crisp, cloudless air; snow-capped peaks; lakes and forests; the sun bright and high in the deep blue sky; and impossible roads that twist and turn their way up shockingly steep gradients: mountains have always exerted a magical power over cyclists.

Plucky, pioneering cycle tourists went first, and racers followed in their tyre tracks. Anyone who's sweated and struggled up a really big hill knows how the pain and suffering quickly evaporates in the breathless, endorphin-drenched euphoria of reaching the top. Britain has no mountains that compare with the Alps or the Pyrenees, but on a fine summer's day the hills around the town of Bala in the southern corner of the Snowdonia National Park are as close as you can get this side of the English Channel.

Bala sits on the shores of Llyn Tegid, Wales's highest natural lake, and it feels very Welsh, from the heavy stone architecture to the Methodist chapel around every corner. Four out of five residents speak Welsh fluently. The long, wide main street and the narrow side streets are lined with independent shops, and their attractive shopfronts date from the time when Bala was a centre for the production of gloves, stockings, flannel and hosiery. Like many other market towns in Wales and the borders, Bala has resisted the march of the chain-dominated 'clone town'. Long may it prosper.

The ride begins with an ascent of Cwm Hirnant. The first village on the route is Rhos-y-gwaliau and the fields downstream of the village have a special place in rural history. Here, in 1873, ten sheepdogs competed before an audience of several hundred spectators in the first recorded sheepdog trial. Beyond the village, the lane climbs through pine forests that line the steep valley.

Out of the forest, the road rounds a bend and the finale of the climb is revealed: a narrow road cut into the heather-covered hillside that continues all the way up to the pass. After crossing the boundary of the National Park it's a high speed, pine-scented descent to the shores of Lake Vyrnwy.

Vyrnwy was the first of Wales's upland valleys to be dammed and flooded to provide a water supply to the teeming cities of Victorian England. In Vyrnwy's case it's the homes and factories of Liverpool. The 11 mile circuit of the lake may well be the longest flat road in the whole of

———

START & FINISH: Bala • DISTANCE: 34 miles/54km • TOTAL ASCENT: 1144m • TERRAIN: Lanes. Challenging

Wales and provides some respite after the big climb. At the far end is the dam, a dark wall of giant blocks of Welsh slate. Completed in 1888, it was a world first as a stone dam; in all previous dams the water was held back by massive earth embankments. The coniferous forests that fringe the lake act as a natural filtration system for the water draining into the reservoir. In the years since, some of the trees have grown into mighty specimens, including a Douglas Fir that was the tallest tree in England and Wales, reaching 63.7 metres until it was damaged in a storm in 2011. About a quarter of it remains as a stump, the top carved into an enormous hand by chainsaw artist Simon O'Rourke.

From the shores of Lake Vyrnwy at Pont Eunant the route continues uphill on a lonely mountain road, past tumbling waterfalls and shady pools perfect for a dip. It's a lovely little route and crafty too, as it gets you almost all the way to the summit of one of the most challenging road climbs in Britain. Bwlch y Groes means 'Pass of the Cross' and any fan of the Tour de France will immediately think of its celebrated Alpine counterpart, the Col de la Croix de Fer. It really is a shockingly steep gradient and it has 11 chevrons on the OS map, more than any other British road. Early motor car manufacturers called the road Hellfire Pass and used it to test prototypes. The road featured in the Milk Race, a precursor to the Tour of Britain, during the 1970s and 80s.

After taking in the views from the top, it's a long, joyful descent down Cwm Cynllwyd and a flat run along the shore of Llyn Tegid back to Bala.

Download route info at thebikeshow.net/06AA

PUBS & PIT STOPS

LAKEVIEW TEA ROOM. Llanwddyn SY10 0ND (01691 870286) Traditional, family-run tea room with a cracking view.

THE OLD BARN CAFÉ, Llanwddyn SY10 0NA (01691 870377) Café just below the Vyrnwy dam (bike hire available).

BRYNIAU GOLAU, Llangower, LL23 7BT (01678 521782) Boutique B&B overlooking Lake Bala.

PANT-YR-ONNEN. Llangower, LL23 7BT (01743 718283) Campsite on Lake Bala with private beach.

BIKE SHOP: R. H. Roberts Cycles, 7-9 High Street, Bala LL23 7AG (01678 520252) Bike hire available.

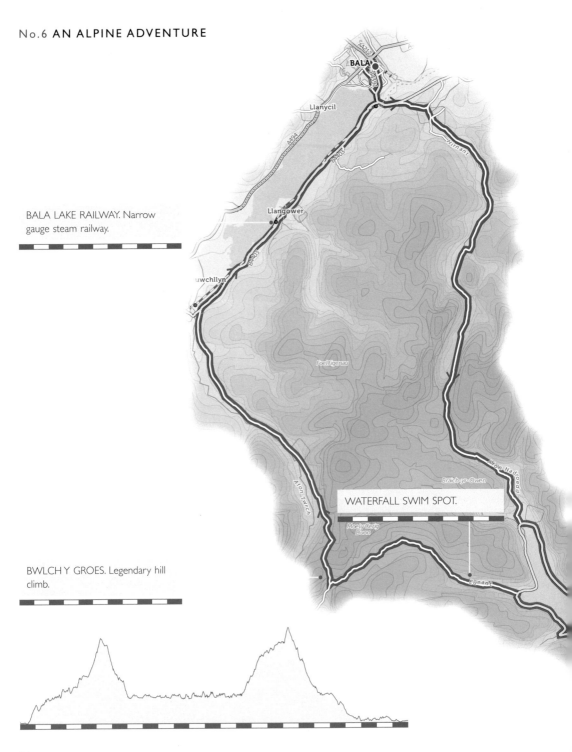

BALA LAKE RAILWAY. Narrow gauge steam railway.

BWLCH Y GROES. Legendary hill climb.

WATERFALL SWIM SPOT.

GIANTS OF VYRNWY TRAIL. Walk among of Britain's tallest trees.

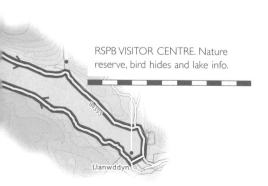

RSPB VISITOR CENTRE. Nature reserve, bird hides and lake info.

Llanwddyn

SEASIDE TO SUBLIME

Ride in the footsteps of the Romantics on one of Wales's best traffic-free cycle paths, with a thrilling return journey on the lower slopes of the mighty Cadair Idris

---

The remote fishing village of Barmouth rose to 19th century prominence as a seaside resort. The Shelleys, Wordsworth, Tennyson and Charles Darwin all came here, drawn by the wild and dramatic location on steep cliffs fringed by mountains with fine views out to sea and a long sandy beach. Barmouth grew into a popular destination for holidaymakers from the Midlands but, though it's a far cry from resorts like Blackpool or Skegness, there is not much left of the atmosphere that attracted the early Victorian visitors. Much less altered is the surrounding countryside. John Ruskin – who knew a thing or two about beauty and the landscape – said there was "no better walk" than up the Mawddach estuary from Barmouth to Dolgellau. Since that time a railway has come and gone and the line now makes for a flat, traffic-free cycling and walking path that's supremely scenic and justly popular, especially among families.

This is a ride of two halves: a gentle spin up the estuary path to Dolgellau followed by a mountain odyssey on the lower slopes of Cadair Idris. It begins with a crossing of the broad Mawddach estuary on Barmouth Bridge, a long wooden bridge originally built for the railway. The Mawddach Trail is easy to follow and offers great views north across the water to the remote rocky outcrops of the Rhinogydd (anglicised as Rhinogs). Eventually, leaving the estuary behind, a tree-lined track crosses the marshes to Dolgellau.

Though people have lived in the valley for thousands of years, Dolgellau itself grew up in the medieval era as a *maerdref*, a township inhabited by serfs who were effectively 'owned' by local princes or chieftains. Under the Tudor kings the town developed into a centre for the weaving of wool and tanning of hides. In the 19th century North Wales experienced a brief gold rush and Dolgellau was its epicentre. Many of the town's dark and sturdy granite and slate buildings date from these heady, prosperous times. More recently the town has become something of an outdoor activity destination as well as playing host to the annual *Sesiwn Fawr* (Big Session), a festival of folk and roots music. It's a good place to stop for lunch as there are no refreshments available once the road heads up towards Cadair Idris, following National Cycle Route 82.

The first mile of the climb is the steepest and after that initial shock to the system the gradient slowly eases. There are dry stone walls lining the lane and marking out intricate field boundaries up the hillsides, and they are exceptionally well laid. As the farms and broadleaf woods give way to more rugged moorland, the rocky giant rising steeply to the left really starts to make its presence

---

START & FINISH: Barmouth • DISTANCE: 27 miles/43km • TOTAL ASCENT: 868m
TERRAIN: Lanes and a gravel cycle track. Moderate

Mawddach Trail

felt. Cadair Idris is a mountain suffused with legend: the lake near the top, it is said, is bottomless; anyone who spends a night on the summit will come back a madman or a poet (one summer solstice I gave it a go but sadly awoke much the same person, if a little sleep-deprived).

After a flattish plateau there's a final push to the pass, then the route makes a right turn towards Cregennan Lakes. The concentration of standing stones and other Bronze Age artefacts suggest this plateau could have been a ceremonial site or, at the very least, a staging post on an important long-distance trackway.

Just past the lakes is a landscape reveal with serious wow factor: a truly bird's eye view of Barmouth and the coastline. It's then a white-knuckle descent down twisting farm lanes to the main road at Arthog and back onto the Mawddach Trail, crossing the long wooden bridge into Barmouth as the setting sun dips over the glittering waters of Cardigan Bay.

Download route info at thebikeshow.net/07SS

PUBS & PIT STOPS

GEORGE III HOTEL, Penmaenpool LL40 1YD (01341 422525) Big, well-appointed waterside hotel, bar and restaurant.

T. H. ROBERTS, Glyndwr St, Dolgellau LL40 1BB (01341 423552) Friendly, atmospheric café in a former ironmonger's shop.

Y SOSPAN, Queens Square, Dolgellau LL40 1AW (01341 423174) Oak-beamed bistro and tea rooms in a 17th century courthouse.

CROSS KEYS, Mill Street, Dolgellau LL40 1EY (01341 423342) Good honest, North Wales boozer.

GWERNAN HOTEL, Islawrdref LL40 1TL (01341 422488) Stylishly appointed six-room country hotel on the slopes of Cadair Idris.

GRAIG WEN, Arthog LL39 1YP (01341 250482) B&B, yurts and chilled-out campsite in a gorgeous spot on the Mawddach Estuary.

KNICKERBOCKERS Church Street, Barmouth LL42 1EW (01341 280133) Colourful ice cream parlour.

BIKE HIRE: Birmingham Garage, Dolgellau Road, Barmouth LL42 1EL (01341 280644)

Dolgellau Cycles, Smithfield Street Dolgellau LL40 1DE (01341 423332)

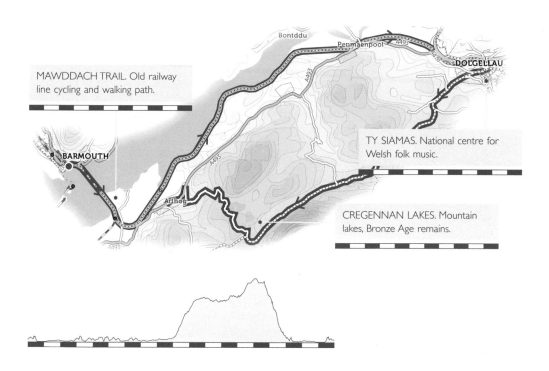

MAWDDACH TRAIL. Old railway line cycling and walking path.

TY SIAMAS. National centre for Welsh folk music.

CREGENNAN LAKES. Mountain lakes, Bronze Age remains.

Cregennan Lakes

No.8

OVER THE TOP

An unforgettable pass-storming adventure across the Berwyn range followed by a gentle run along the Dee valley

---

Mountain biking, so the story goes, was invented by a gang of hippies in 1970s Marin County, California. In plaid shirts, ripped jeans and sporting extravagant facial hair, they raced heavy beach cruisers with coaster brakes down steep, rough, mountain tracks. Among them were the likes of Gary Fisher, Tom Ritchey and Joe Breeze, who became big names in the mountain bike boom of the 1980s. But off-road cycling actually goes back much further, to the very earliest days of the bicycle.

In Britain this kind of riding has traditionally been known as 'rough stuff' and this ride includes a classic rough stuff route first popularised in an article in *Cycling* magazine way back in 1919. The author was cycling journalist Walter M. Robinson, better known by his pen name Wayfarer, and he describes riding across the Berwyn mountain range in March, when it was still snowbound. Battling against inclement weather and arduous terrain, he was often forced to push or even carry his bike, but concludes that "some of the best of cycling would be missed if one always had to be in the saddle or on a hard road".

The ride starts right on the England-Wales border at Chirk, following a relatively quiet B road up the Ceiriog valley, passing beneath the stout walls of Chirk Castle, built shortly after Edward I's conquest of North Wales. More than a century earlier, it was in this steep-sided, thickly wooded valley that the invading army of Edward I's great-grandfather Henry II were routed by the allied forces of the Welsh princes.

Llanarmon Dyffryn Ceiriog is a small village that lies on the Ceiriog river and at the junction of three major drovers' roads. This explains the presence of a pair of sizeable inns in a small, remote upland village. The village – and the whole valley – was to have been flooded as part of a reservoir project to supply water to the town of Warrington (similar schemes had already flooded the Vyrnwy, Elan and Alwen valleys). Local people and their representatives in Parliament argued fiercely against "drowning Wales to slake the thirst of Englishmen". In the end the project was dropped and the valley, described by former Prime Minister David Lloyd-George as a "little piece of heaven on earth", was saved.

The tarmac road continues beyond Llanarmon for a mile or two before giving way to a rough track. Here the fun begins and – depending on the weather, the condition of the track, your tyres, gears and moral fibre – it will be a mixture of riding and pushing all the way up to Bwlch Nant Rhyd Wilym, the pass at the summit crest. It was here, in 1957, that the founding members of the Rough Stuff Fellowship (a group devoted to off-road adventure cycling) installed a small memorial to Wayfarer, their hero. It's now accompanied by a weatherproof box containing

---

START & FINISH: Chirk • DISTANCE: 43 miles/69km • TOTAL ASCENT: 1338m
TERRAIN: Lanes, a long, unsurfaced mountain track and canal towpath. Very Challenging

Pont-Cysylite aqueduct

Valle Crucis Abbey

bound notebooks in which passers-by can share their thoughts. It's a varied anthology, with a thoughtful ode to the landscape on one page and a cartoon penis on the next.

On the run down the other side, the views across the valley of the River Dee are superb, and the track is shorter and easier going than on the way up. Even so, the tarmac comes as quite a relief. From the valley floor at Cynwyd it's a couple of flat miles to Corwen. Though it has a long history and a close association with Owain Glyndŵr, last native prince of Wales, the town feels down on its luck. Having the A5 go straight through the main street hasn't helped. It's a fast, busy road but for the journey east towards Llangollen there's a terrific lost lane alternative on the north bank of the River Dee.

Just before Llangollen it's a short, stiff climb up onto a mountain road past the medieval ruins of Castell Dinas Brân (if legs are tired, the alternative is to take the canal towpath through Llangollen).

Descending through Garth to Trevor, the final section of the ride is along the canal towpath all the way back to Chirk, starting with the vertigo-inducing Pontcysyllte aqueduct, a wonder of the industrial revolution, which carries the Llangollen Canal across the River Dee.

Wayfarer's original article describing his crossing of the Berwyns was entitled 'Over the Top', a military allusion that would have resonated with his readers. Many of them had experienced the horrors of trench warfare and all would have lost friends and family in the Great War. By repurposing the phrase 'over the top' to describe an off-road bike adventure, Wayfarer was tapping into people's desire to put war behind them, to get out into the open air and rediscover their country – on foot, by bike and, in the case of a ride like this, a bit of both.

Download route info at thebikeshow.net/08OT

PUBS & PIT STOPS

THE HAND, Llanarmon Dyffryn Ceiriog LL20 7LD (01691 600666) Lovely country inn with excellent food.

WEST ARMS HOTEL, Llanarmon Dyffryn Ceiriog LL20 7LD (01691 600665) Historic drovers inn. Wayfarers Bar at the back. Rooms available.

THE GROUSE INN, Carrog LL21 9AT (01490 430272) Friendly riverside pub with good, simple food served all day.

THE SUN INN, Rhewl, LL20 7YT (01978 860860) Tiny drovers' inn serving beer from the local Llangollen microbrewery.

PROSPECT TEA ROOMS, Blackwood Road, Garth LL20 7YL. (01978 821602) Cottage tea rooms, fine views.

TELFORD INN, Trevor Basin LL20 7TT. (01978 820469) Sunny pub before the Pontcysyllte Aqueduct.

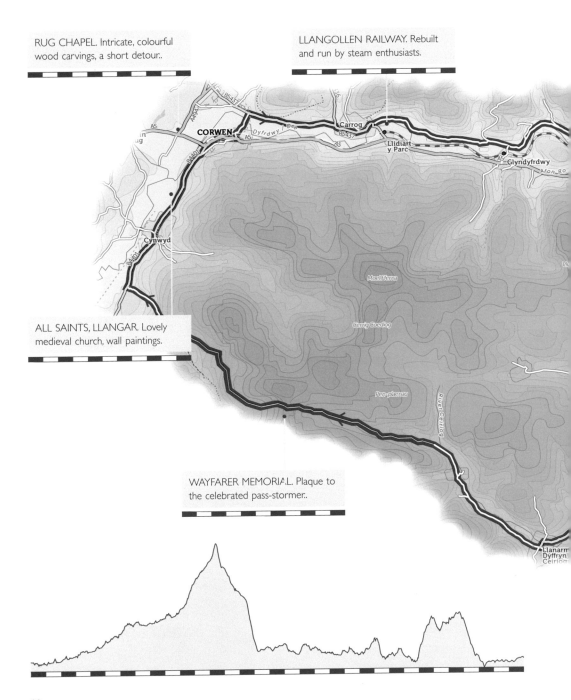

RUG CHAPEL. Intricate, colourful wood carvings, a short detour..

LLANGOLLEN RAILWAY. Rebuilt and run by steam enthusiasts.

ALL SAINTS, LLANGAR. Lovely medieval church, wall paintings.

WAYFARER MEMORIAL. Plaque to the celebrated pass-stormer..

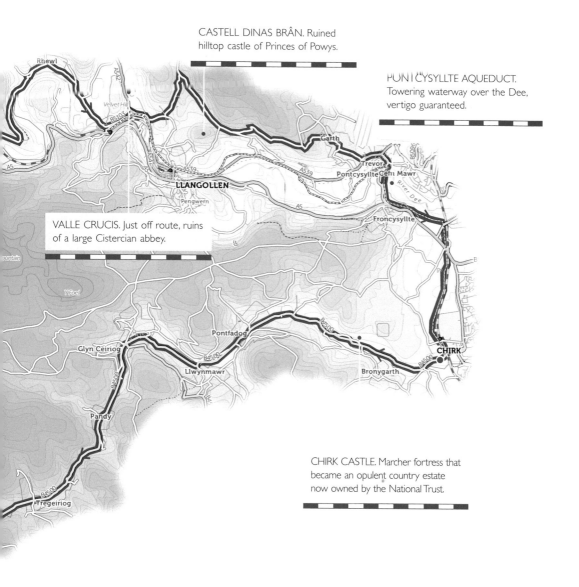

CASTELL DINAS BRÂN. Ruined hilltop castle of Princes of Powys.

PONTCYSYLLTE AQUEDUCT. Towering waterway over the Dee, vertigo guaranteed.

VALLE CRUCIS. Just off route, ruins of a large Cistercian abbey.

CHIRK CASTLE. Marcher fortress that became an opulent country estate now owned by the National Trust.

River Dee

MID
WALES

WOOL, WIND AND WOOD

From Machynlleth into the secluded foothills of the Cambrian mountains
and a return along the banks of the Dyfi

———

The wild mouflon of Mesopotamia is a large-horned goat-like beast with short, wiry brown hair. It was one of the first species of wild animals to be domesticated, more than 10,000 years ago. Sheep, as they would become, first came to Britain with the Romans. Until the 20th century and the advent of synthetic fibres, sheep were bred more for their wool and milk than for their meat, and wool was the foundation of the medieval economy.

Traditionally the Welsh uplands were grazed by cattle but their place has now largely been taken by sheep. There are now eight million sheep in Wales, per head of population more than anywhere else in the world (even New Zealand currently). Yet most sheep farms are loss-making businesses that rely on subsidies from the European Union. And they're not only a burden on taxpayers – the swathes of hill country grazed so heavily they resemble bowling greens come at an environmental cost: deforestation, soil erosion and landslips, flash flooding in the valleys below and the loss of plant and animal species. This has led the journalist George Monbiot to describe the landscape of mid-Wales as "sheep-wrecked" and to call into question Wales's national affection for the "white maggots" that "plague" the Cambrian mountains.

This ride begins in Machynlleth, the arty market town on the River Dovey. Here, in 1404,

Owain Glyndŵr was crowned as the last Welsh-born Prince of Wales. He convened a parliament in a barn-like hall house that now houses a museum to the man who became a symbol of Welsh nationalism and resistance to English rule. The town is also home to Wales's Museum of Modern Art and, just out of town, the Centre for Alternative Technology.

This is hill country and it's a hilly ride, though the climbing is heavily front-loaded for when legs are freshest because the second half of the ride is a long, lovely roll along the Afon Dyfi. To begin, the route follows the Afon Dulas on National Cycle Route 8, turning north through the hamlets of Melinbyrhedyn and Tal-y-Wern. Simon Jenkins, another journalist with an interest in Welsh affairs, has described the twin curses of mid-Wales as caravans and conifers. On the 200-metre climb up to Bwlch Glynmynydd there's plenty of the latter: gloomy, lifeless plantations that, when felled, resemble post-apocalyptic war zones.

It's a fast descent to Llanbrynmair, a village that was once known as Wynnstay, named after the largest of the landed estates that dominated the economics and politics of rural Wales for centuries. Up until the last 100 years or so, most Welsh farmers were tenants and lived under the threat of eviction if they stood up to their

---

START & FINISH: Machynlleth • DISTANCE: 34 miles/54km • TOTAL ASCENT: 933m
TERRAIN: Lanes. Challenging

landlords, who demanded not only rent but the votes of their tenants in elections to parliament. Along with a desire for freedom of religion, it was a hunger for land that spurred many rural Welsh to emigrate to the United States, and Llanbrynmair is said to have seen a higher proportion of the population emigrate than any other part of Wales, many finding their new lives in the state of Ohio.

North of Llanbrynmair is a glorious lost lane, climbing gently through another valley that, come spring, is filled with sheep. The ewes and their lambs often mistake an approaching cyclist for the farmer bearing their next meal, their imploring bleating reaching a tragic crescendo as you pass by. Most of the time it's difficult to identify with these dumb, devil-eyed creatures, apparently indifferent to the cold and impervious to rain, but I always find the sight of a shaggy ewe tenderly nursing its gangly-legged offspring to be deeply moving, one species of mammal regarding another. It's then a real pang of conflicted emotions the next time I find myself tucking into a juicy chop. At least the lambs, though they rarely live more than a year, spend their time outdoors and in comparative liberty.

Way up high at the top of the valley are the stark white turbines of the wind farm on the summit plateau of Mynydd Cemais. Wind power is big business in mid-Wales and divides local communities. Some welcome the new jobs and the contribution to renewable energy; others see turbines as blots on wild upland landscapes and worry about the impact on wildlife, both from the turbines and the overhead power lines that connect them to the national grid. As with sheep farming and forestry, politics is at the heart of wind power, both through decisions about land use and the subsidies that make wind power economically viable.

From the top of the climb it's downhill almost all the way back to Machynlleth, initially on the A458 to Mallwyd, then on a quiet lane on the north bank of the Dyfi. This was once slate quarrying country and many of the older buildings in the valley, as well as gravestones, are made from slate. A couple of miles past Cemmaes the lane joins the B4404 for the final run to the new cycling and walking bridge and the cycle path into Machynlleth.

Download route info at thebikeshow.net/09WW

PUBS & PIT STOPS

WYNNSTAY ARMS, Llanbrynmair SY19 7AA (01650 521431) 300 year old pub and B&B, needs a little TLC.

CAFE DRAIG, The Old Village Hall, Llanbrynmair SY19 7AA (01650 521552) Bright, airy café amid the mechanical toys with a view of the rabbit village.

BRIGANDS INN, Mallwyd SY20 9HJ (01650 511 999) Big old coaching in remodelled into an upmarket dining pub with rooms.

PENRHOS ARMS HOTEL, Cemmaes SY20 9PR (01650 511 243) Stone-built pub with B&B and restaurant.

QUARRY CAFE, 13 Maengwyn Street, Machynlleth SY20 8EB (01654 702424) Vegetarian café popular with locals.

NUMBER TWENTY-ONE, 21 Maengwyn Street, Machynlleth SY20 8EB (01654 703382) Gourmet bistro, local food.

HENNIGAN'S, 123 Maengwyn Street, Machynlleth SY20 8EF (01654) 702761. Award-winning fish and chips to take away.

Y FELIN, Melinbyrhedyn SY20 8SJ (01654 702718) Tiny, idyllic campsite on a permaculture farm.

GWALIA FARM, Cemmaes SY20 9PZ (01650 511377). Peaceful, rustic camping & glamping on an organic smallholding.

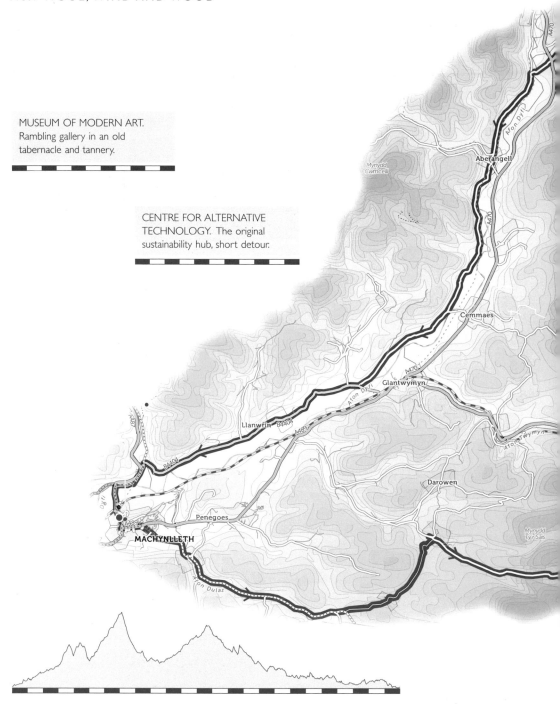

MUSEUM OF MODERN ART.
Rambling gallery in an old
tabernacle and tannery.

CENTRE FOR ALTERNATIVE
TECHNOLOGY. The original
sustainability hub, short detour.

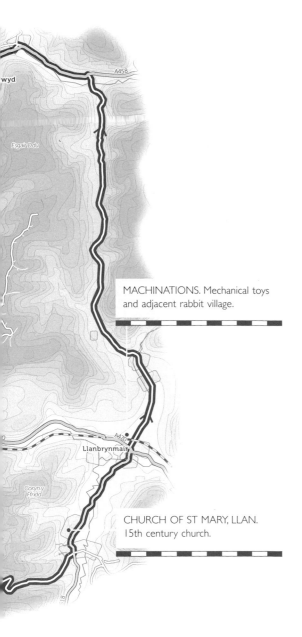

MACHINATIONS. Mechanical toys and adjacent rabbit village.

CHURCH OF ST MARY, LLAN. 15th century church.

THE GREEN DESERT

Into Wales's vast emptiness for a ride along the Elan valley's chain of sparkling lakes

---

I once spent a long, cloudless midsummer day in the heart of the Cambrian mountains and managed to ride until five in the afternoon before I saw anyone else on a bike. It was near the top of the climb west from Rhayader up the Nant Gwynllyn valley. The craggy, middle-aged rider coming the other way wore no helmet, was sporting bright yellow 1980s-style Oakley sunglasses, a big tattoo and was riding a hand-built titanium road bike. There was no mistaking British cycling legend Sean Yates, one of the few domestic riders to have worn the coveted yellow jersey in the Tour de France. As a racer, Sean had a lot in common with the Elenydd, the windswept moorland plateau in the heart of the Cambrian range where our paths crossed. Both are gritty and unglamorous, somewhat shy of the limelight and tough as old boots.

This route starts in Rhayader and follows the same climb up to Penrhiw-wen and down to the bridge over the Elan river. The road west from here goes over the mountains to the Ystwyth valley and all the way to the coast at Aberystwyth (that's where Sean had ridden from that day), but this ride turns left over the bridge and continues along the western bank of the Craig Goch reservoir. This is the highest of the four reservoirs that drowned the Elan valley in the 1890s as part of an ambitious, state-of-the-art scheme to supply fresh water to Birmingham. The giant Claerwen reservoir, in the neighbouring valley, was added around 50 years later. During the construction phase it was used by the Royal Air Force for testing the bouncing bombs used in the Dambusters raid on Nazi Germany. The Elan valley reservoirs and their dams, built in their distinctive 'Birmingham baroque' style, have their own eerie magnificence, but are nothing compared to the beautiful landscape that was lost.

Percy Bysshe Shelley stayed here with his uncle, who was the squire at Cwm Elan, a large house in the valley. The young Shelley penned rapturous verse inspired by his long rambles: "When mountain, meadow, wood and stream / With unalloying glory gleam / And to the spirit's ear and eye / Are unison and harmony." In 1812 he moved to a neighbouring valley and tried to make a home here with his young wife, Harriet Westbrook. Their love story did not have a happy ending. They separated and Harriet drowned herself in the Serpentine, aged just 21. A few years later Shelley himself drowned – by accident – off the coast of Italy, aged 29. It is a gothic irony that their own watery deaths were followed by the inundation of the valley where they lived and loved, lost to the rising waters along with 18 farms, three manor houses, a church, a mill and a school.

START & FINISH: Rhayader • DISTANCE: 22 miles/35km • TOTAL ASCENT: 737m
TERRAIN: Lanes, optional unsurfaced cycle tracks. Moderate

Despite the sadness of the flooded valleys, the series of dams is undeniably an astonishing feat of engineering and they are at their most spectacular when in spate, with foaming whitewater cascading down their steep faces. The dams were built by a workforce of up to a thousand navvies, who were initially housed in makeshift wooden villages and later at the purpose-built Elan Village. The water flows by pipe and aqueduct for 73 miles to the city of Birmingham; the journey is powered by gravity alone and takes a day and a half.

At the first dam, Craig Goch, there is a choice to be made. The surfaced road continues along the western shore of the next reservoir, Pen-y-garreg, but on the far side of the dam there's an off-road cycle path through some lovely broadleaf woodland. Likewise, the next reservoir, Garreg Ddu, has both a surfaced road and a traffic-free cycle track. Unless you have very thin tyres or it's really foul weather, the cycle track is preferable, not least because it's flatter and closer to the water's edge.

At Caban Coch, the fourth and final dam, rather than follow National Cycle Route 81 straight down the valley, make a short but intensely scenic detour along the Dulas valley. It's a truly lost lane that might give a hint of how the Elan valley looked before it was flooded. The last stretch along the Wye valley culminates in a final crossing of the Elan river on the Glyn Bridge, a rickety suspension footbridge just before the river flows into the Wye. It's then a mile across the floodplain back to Rhayader.

Download route info at thebikeshow.net/10GD

PUBS & PIT STOPS

PENBONT TEAROOM, Elan Valley LD6 5HS (01597 811515) Light lunches and traditional teas in lovely setting by the Pen y Garreg Dam. One room B&B.

ELAN VALLEY VISITOR CENTRE, Elan Valley LD6 5HP (01597 810880) Café with views of the Caban Coch Dam. Bike hire available.

THE TRIANGLE INN, Cwmdauddwr LD6 5AR (01597 810537) Old drovers inn on the edge of Rhayader.

TY MORGAN'S. EAST STREET, Rhayader LD6 5DS (01597 811666) Smart café, bed and breakfast.

OLD SWAN TEA ROOMS. West Street, Rhayader LD6 5AB (01597 811060) Cheerful little café and cake shop.

BIKE SHOP: Elan Cycles. West St, Rhayader, Powys LD6 5AB. Bike shop and café run by former top bike racer Clive Powell.

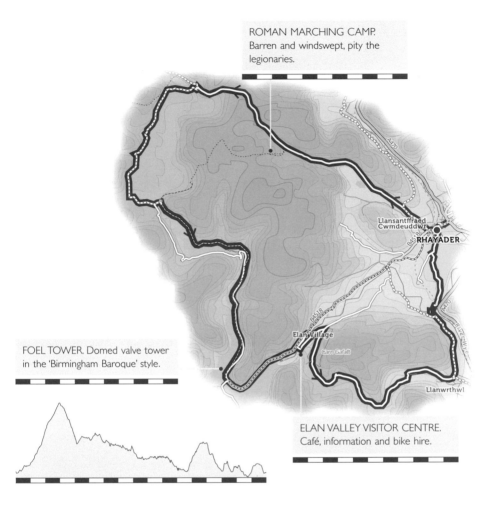

ROMAN MARCHING CAMP.
Barren and windswept, pity the
legionaries.

FOEL TOWER. Domed valve tower
in the 'Birmingham Baroque' style.

ELAN VALLEY VISITOR CENTRE.
Café, information and bike hire.

No.11

LLANDOVERY DISCOVERY

A revivalist ramble through deepest Carmarthenshire in the isolated hills above the River Towy

———

There's a joke about a shipwrecked Welshman marooned on a desert island. After many long years he is spotted by a passing ship and the crew are amazed to find the island is covered in fine buildings that he has built himself. With pride, the Welsh Robinson Crusoe takes the ship's captain on a tour of the island, pointing out his house, the pub, the rugby ground and two chapels. "Why *two* chapels?" asks the captain. "Well you see," he replies, "that's the chapel I go to and that's the chapel I don't".

The joke hinges on the strength of nonconformist religions in Wales and their bewildering diversity. Rooted in Welsh language and culture and putting the congregation at the centre of affairs, Nonconformism offered an attractive homegrown alternative to the hidebound, arcane rituals of the Church of England. Though rural in origin, Nonconformism really took hold in the towns and cities of the industrial south. In the first half of the 19th century, a new chapel opened every eight days and ministers were the rock stars of the times.

Combining social conservatism (abstinence from alcohol) with a democratic, anti-establishment radicalism (support for free trade, workers' rights and free education), the impact of chapel on Welsh politics, society and culture is felt to this day. There are more than 5,000 chapels in Wales, ranging from small, humble 'tin tabernacles' to grandiose, architecturally dazzling urban edifices. It's common for even the smallest village to have two, three or even four chapels.

The 20th century saw chapel attendance collapse and many are left empty and dilapidated, a vivid symbol of changing values. This ride, a circuit of the remote, sparsely populated massif of Mynydd Mallaen at the southern tip of the Cambrian Mountains, takes in two of the oldest rural chapels in Wales along with some classic, rugged mid-Wales countryside.

In a description that still holds true, the Victorian travel writer George Borrow recalled Llandovery as "about the pleasantest little town in which I have halted in the course of my wanderings". The Romans built a large fort here, the Normans added a castle, and the numerous pubs are a reminder of the town's history as a centre of the drovers' trade.

The route first heads north, crossing the River Towy at Dolauhirion Bridge on a quiet lane that was once the main coach road from Llandovery to Lampeter. Built in 1773, I'd say the bridge is one of the world's most beautiful, right up there with the Rialto in Venice and the Golden Gate in California.

START & FINISH: Llandovery • DISTANCE: 28 miles/44km • TOTAL ASCENT: 797m
TERRAIN: Lanes. Moderate

Capel Bwlch-y-Rhiw

The Black Mountain

The first village on the route is Cilycwm and the Soar Chapel is about half a mile east, on the road to Cynghordy. Built around 1740 it may be the oldest Methodist chapel in Wales. Continuing up the western bank of the Towy as far as Towy Bridge, the left-hand fork follows the lane up Nant Melyn, a steep-sided valley of oak woods and waterfalls. In spring and early summer the valley sparkles with wild flowers.

Just before the pass stands the small, stout, whitewashed form of Capel Bwlch-y-Rhiw. It is one of the oldest Baptist chapels in Wales and was built in 1717 by a group of Baptists and Congregationalists who, at a time when Nonconformists suffered widespread persecution, had been forced to worship in secret, meeting in a nearby cave and in a smithy close to the site of the present chapel. Baptists believe in baptism by total immersion and there is an adult-sized baptismal pool next to the stream, fed by freezing water straight off the mountain.

From the pass it's a long, gentle descent down the Cothi valley as far as the gold mines at Dolaucothi. These are the only known Roman gold mines in Britain, though gold prospecting in the gravels of the Afon Cothi may date back to the Bronze Age. The mines were briefly revived by the Victorians before closing for good in 1938 and the site is now owned and run by the National Trust.

The next section is a steep ramp up to Caio, then a rollercoaster ride through Porthyryd to Siloh. On the final downhill stretch back to Llandovery there are fine views across the Towy valley to the unmistakably angular and brooding form of the Black Mountain.

Download route info at thebikeshow.net/11LD

PUBS & PIT STOPS

NEUADD FAWR ARMS, Cilycwm SA20 0ST (01550 721644) Great village pub, excellent food.

TOWY BRIDGE INN, Towy Bridge SA20 0PE (01550 760370). Riverside inn, pub grub.

TEA ROOM, Dolaucothi Gold Mines, Pumsaint SA19 8US (01558 650177). National Trust tea room.

BRUNANT ARMS, Church Street, Caio SA19 8RD (01558 650 483) Unpretentious village pub, real ale, simple food.

OLD PRINTING OFFFICE, 1 Broad Street, Llandovery SA20 0AR (01550 720690) Lovely café at the back of a gift shop.

JUST SO SCRUMPTIOUS, 4 Kings Road, Llandovery SA20 0AW (01550 720824) Café and deli, perfect for packing a picnic.

NEW WHITE LION HOTEL, 43 Stone Street, Llandovery SA20 0BZ (01550 720 685) Upscale boutique hotel.

THE DROVERS, 9 Market Square, Llandovery SA20 0AB (01550 721115) Elegant 17th century town house B&B.

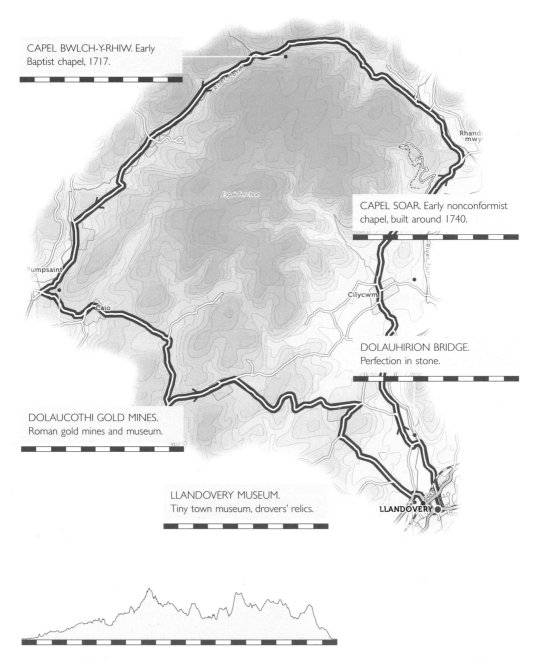

CAPEL BWLCH-Y-RHIW. Early Baptist chapel, 1717.

CAPEL SOAR. Early nonconformist chapel, built around 1740.

DOLAUHIRION BRIDGE. Perfection in stone.

DOLAUCOTHI GOLD MINES. Roman gold mines and museum.

LLANDOVERY MUSEUM. Tiny town museum, drovers' relics.

LLANDOVERY

Pumpsaint

Caio

Cilycwm

Esgair Ferchon

Rhandi mwyi

Dolauhirion Bridge

Llandovery

WATERY WALES

A mostly easygoing exploration of the southern tip of the Cambrian mountains, with some inviting wild swim spots along the way

———

The year was 1732 and Theophilus Evans, a priest and man of letters, was suffering from an attack of the scurvy. He had heard tell of an evil-smelling spring in his parish, on the banks of the River Irfon, and so the ailing curate set out to find it, hoping that the sulphurous waters might possess curative powers. The spring was a little upstream of a tiny hamlet named Pont-Rhyd-y-Fferau (Bridge over the ankle-deep ford). After two months of taking the mineral-rich waters Evans had made a dramatic recovery.

Word spread and people flocked to this remote mid-Wales valley. With the sudden influx of visitors, the hamlet near the spring grew into a small town and was rechristened Llanwrtyd Wells, a spa town to rival nearby Llandrindod and Builth Wells. The railway came in the 1860s, bringing yet more visitors. At the height of its fame Llanwrtyd Wells was a bustling resort with hotels, cafés, tennis courts and a grand, tree-lined avenue leading to ornate pavilions and bath houses around the spring.

Not much survives of the town's late-Victorian glory, but Llanwrtyd Wells has had to reinvent itself, first by pioneering the outdoor pursuit of pony trekking and more recently as Britain's capital of silly sports and wacky races. The longest running events are the man versus horse marathon and the world

bog snorkelling championships. Bog snorkelling is a sporting pursuit that takes place in a six-foot-deep trench filled with muddy water. There is a mountain bike variant where riders compete on a specially adapted bike with a lead-filled frame and water-filled tyres. The annual World Alternative Games held in and around the town now comprises 60 disciplines, including worm charming, sack fighting and Russian egg roulette.

This ride doesn't involve any bog snorkelling but it does have quite a watery feel to it, as it traces the winding course of the River Irfon and two of its tributaries. This means hills are kept to a minimum and there are some good spots for a paddle or a dip.

From Llanwrtyd Wells the route follows the Irfon downstream along hedge-lined lanes through rolling pasture and some fine coppiced woodland. The range of hills away to the southwest is the Mynydd Epynt, a remote upland plateau once home to a sparse Welsh-speaking hill farming community. In 1940 the area was requisitioned by the military and 200 people were evicted from their homes. The Sennybridge Training Area is the third largest military training base in the country, covering about the same area as the island of Jersey. It is complete with fake farmsteads, mock hedgerows and the odd-looking conifer plantations that, from

---

START & FINISH: Llanwrtyd Wells • DISTANCE: 18 miles/29km • TOTAL ASCENT: 485m
TERRAIN: Lanes. Easy

a distance, seem like huge dark green caterpillars crawling all over the massif.

A few miles on, a left turn down a short track leads to a footbridge over the Afon Irfon. The footbridge is modern but the ford beside it is definitely ancient. This has been a river crossing at least as far back as Roman times as it lies on the course of the Roman road between Carmarthen and Llandrindod Wells. After crossing the river, the ride carries on along the Roman road towards the ruins of a Roman fort just outside Beulah. From here the route begins to head up gently on a quiet lane that clings to the southern flank of the Cnyffiad valley, through woods that in late spring are a haze of bluebells. Below, on the valley floor, sheep and cattle graze.

The lane passes the Coed Trallwm mountain bike trails centre and shortly after the pass at 332 metres, in a wide bowl at the head of the valley, sits the small village of Abergwesyn. The village is at the junction with the long mountain road west to Tregaron. Three miles along the road from Abergwesyn is the Devil's Staircase, a fearsome and celebrated hill climb that has featured in countless bike races – it's so steep that even top professional riders have been forced to get off and walk.

It's an altogether more leisurely ride back to Llanwrtyd Wells, following the clear waters of the Irfon as they rush and tumble down the valley. There is a handful of wild swimming spots along the way. The biggest is the Washpool, a wide, deep pool that was once used by drovers to wash their sheep. The water here is clear and cool and the pine-scented air smells a lot better than the sulphurous stench of the springs that first brought fame and fortune to the upper Irfon valley.

Download route info at thebikeshow.net/12WW

PUBS & PIT STOPS

THE TROUT INN, Beulah, LD5 4UU (01591 620235) Cheery pub and B&B.

LLWYN MADOC LD5 4TT (01591 620564) Manor house B&B in the beautiful Cnyffiad valley.

COED TRALLWM LD5 4TS (01591 610546). Café and holiday cottages at cycle trail centre. Sells basic bike spares.

NEUADD ARMS HOTEL, The Square, Llanwrtyd Wells LD5 4RB (01591 610236) Fabulous eccentric hotel & microbrewery.

CARLTON RIVERSIDE, Irfon Crescent, Llanwrtyd Wells LD5 4SP (01591 610248) Restaurant with rooms on the banks of the Irfon.

MOUNTAIN ROAD. Turning for
Devil's Staircase and Wolf's Leap

ST DAVID'S, ABERGWESYN.
Ruined 12th century church.

WASHPOOL.. Wild swim spot.

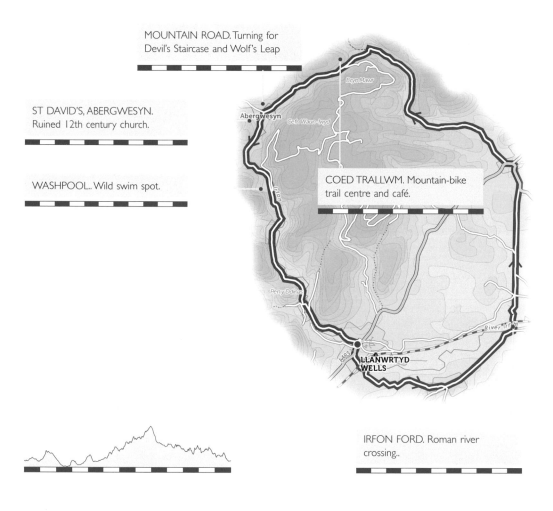

COED TRALLWM. Mountain-bike
trail centre and café.

IRFON FORD. Roman river
crossing..

No.13

KILVERT'S HILLS

A hilly tour of tiny churches in the lost quarter of Radnorshire
on the trail of its most celebrated cleric

———

Francis Kilvert was a country parson in the village of Clyro in the 1870s with a lively, curious mind and a gift for words. He recorded his day-to-day life in voluminous diaries that some regard as second only to those of Samuel Pepys. Kilvert would explore his parish on lengthy rambles around the Black Mountains and Radnorshire hills, tending to his flock and simply enjoying the landscape and his encounters with the people he met along the way. He paints a picture of rural life that seems unimaginably distant a century and a half later. While his diaries make for fascinating reading, there are a few uncomfortable moments too as he describes an unhealthy obsession with a string of underage girls to whose "wild rich nature" he felt "irresistibly drawn".

This ride takes in a little-explored corner of the southern Radnorshire hills which Kilvert would have known very well, calling in on several of the lovely, unadorned rural churches that were the focal points for generations of people who lived out their whole lives in the hills and valleys of an unyielding yet enchanting landscape. It's not a long ride by distance but the hills are many and steep, so it should make for a good day's riding with plenty of stops along the way.

The ride begins in Hay-on-Wye, the groovy border town that's the secondhand bookshop capital of the world and home to Britain's biggest literary festival. The town makes an ideal base for exploring, with plenty of places to eat and drink and an excellent bike shop in Drovers Cycles.

First of all take the B4351 across the Wye to Clyro, from where it's uphill almost immediately on a fabulous farm track that feels like a green lane but is still perfectly rideable and almost totally free of motor traffic. It's an old way that would delight the likes of Robert Macfarlane, and Kilvert would certainly have walked it, casting his long shadow among the gnarled roots and twisted trunks of the wind-whipped hawthorns that line the lane as it climbs Clyro Hill. Turn to savour the view back to Hay before the descent into Rhos-goch and another big climb up to Bryngwyn and then take the lonely mountain road over the top to Glascwm. A very quiet place now, Glascwm was once an ecclesiastical centre, with a Celtic Christian community possibly as far back as the sixth century. The church is much larger than you'd expect in such a small, remote settlement.

After all the hills, the next section following the Clas Brook down to Cregrina is a joy. Smaller than Glascwm, the church at Cregrina crouches hard by the sparkling waters of the River Edw. A little further down the valley, tucked into a narrow valley beneath Red Hill, is the tiny whitewashed church at Rhulen.

START & FINISH: Hay-on-Wye • DISTANCE: 26 miles/41km • TOTAL ASCENT: 1087m
TERRAIN: Lanes. Challenging

It's a contemplative place and it's worth spending a little time taking it all in as there's yet another big climb ahead, up the north flank of Rhulen Hill and onto a wild moorland plateau. Though only 400 metres above sea level, it feels like the roof of the world. On a clear day there are fine views in every direction. The dark, shadowy ridge of the Black Mountains rises in the south, and in the far distance are the peaks of the Brecon Beacons.

It's then a glorious, long descent into Painscastle. Historians believe there's been a fortress here at least since the Roman era, though it was Pain FitzJohn, an Anglo-Norman nobleman, who built the castle that gives the village its name. In early medieval power struggles between the Marcher lords and the Welsh princes the castle was repeatedly besieged, captured, destroyed and rebuilt. A decisive battle in 1198 saw Maud de Braose, the legendary Marcher matriarch commanding the castle, hold out against a besieging Welsh army led by Gwenwynwyn, Prince of Powys. Once her reinforcements arrived, Maud led the massacre of more than 3,000 Welshmen in one of the bloodiest battles in Welsh history.

Years later, Maud herself met a grisly end, imprisoned by King John at Dorset's Corfe Castle along with her son and starved to death. Their ill treatment outraged the English nobility and may have inspired Clause 39 of the Magna Carta, prohibiting imprisonment without trial. It's one of just three clauses that still stands as law today. Centuries later, Painscastle was an important waypoint for drovers, with a half dozen inns as late as the 1860s as well as a 'ha'penny field' where animals were rested on their long journey to London. In Kilvert's time the vicar of Painscastle was John Price, a kindly, Cambridge-educated Anglican priest who was reduced to paying his nonconformist parishioners to attend his services. He lived until his death in a tiny cabin, and Kilvert wrote that "the squalor, the dirt, the dust, the foulness, and wretchedness of the place were indescribable, almost inconceivable."

From Painscastle there is just one last leg-buckling climb left before the descent to Clyro on narrow, wooded back lanes. From here, it's a matter of retracing the short journey from earlier in the day over the River Wye and back to Hay.

Download route info at thebikeshow.net/13KH

PUBS & PIT STOPS

BASKERVILLE ARMS, Clyro HR3 5RZ (01497 820670) Hotel, pub and time warp.

BASKERVILLE HALL, Clyro HR3 5LE (01497 820033) Grand, eccentric country house hotel and bunkhouse with pool and sauna.

HUNDRED HOUSE INN, Hundred House LD1 5RY (01982 570231) Two miles off route, north of Cregina, but the only pub for miles.

ROAST OX INN, Painscastle LD2 3JL (01497 851398) Last of the town's drovers' inns. Good simple food, B&B.

BLUE BOAR, Castle Street, Hay-on-Wye HR3 5DF (01497 820884) Friendly, wood-panelled pub, good food.

RICHARD BOOTH'S BOOKSHOP CAFÉ, 44 Lion Street, Hay-on-Wye HR3 5AA (01497 820322) Hidden café in the King of Hay's book emporium.

KILVERT'S. The Bull-Ring, Hay-on-Wye HR3 5AG (01497 821042) Edwardian former doctor's house turned relaxed, comfortable inn.

BIKE SHOP: Drovers Cycles. Forest Road, Hay-on-Wye HR3 5EH (01497 822419) Bike hire available.

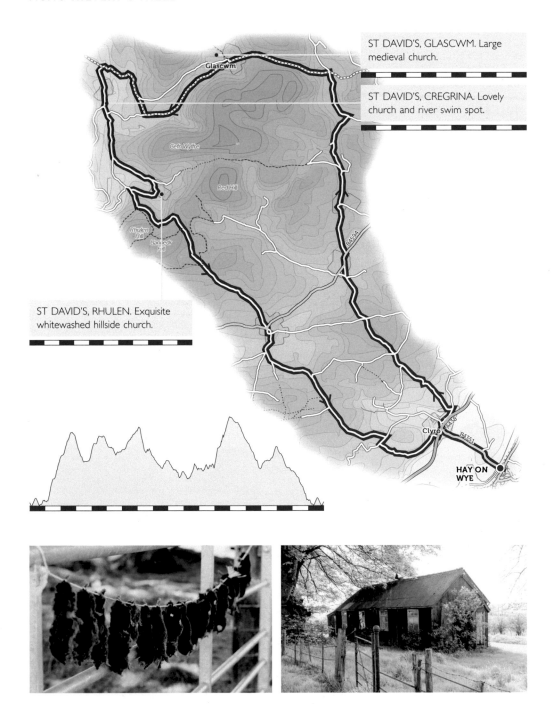

ST DAVID'S, GLASCWM. Large medieval church.

ST DAVID'S, CREGRINA. Lovely church and river swim spot.

ST DAVID'S, RHULEN. Exquisite whitewashed hillside church.

Cregrina Church

Rhulen church

SOUTH
WALES

No.14

AROUND THE BLACK HILL

Up Wales's highest road to the idyllic Vale of Ewyas, returning on the English side of the Black Mountains

———

No part of the 160 mile border between England and Wales is more obviously, undeniably, a fact of the landscape than the eight-mile ridge between Hatterall Hill and Hay Bluff. There was no need for Offa to build a dyke here as nature had done the work for him. It still marks the border between England and Wales. From the east the Black Mountains really do look black: a brooding form silhouetted against the sky. They must have been named by the Saxons, who always looked upon them from the east.

Of all the rides in this book, this may be the one that I cherish most. Not because it's better than any of the others, but because it's a ride I have ridden countless times since moving to the Welsh Borders. Every time it's different yet it's always just the right combination of distance, terrain and scenery to guarantee a glorious day out. It's a loop that can be ridden in either direction but when starting from Hay-on-Wye it makes sense to go anti-clockwise, as this gets the big climb up to Gospel Pass out of the way while the legs are still fresh.

Gospel Pass is Wales's highest paved road and one of the great road climbs in British cycling. It's a full 456 metres in vertical ascent and it really is a scaled-down version of the famed climbs of the Alps and Pyrenees. It begins along narrow farm lanes lined with tall hedgerows then it kicks up dramatically through woodland, before the landscape opens out into a plateau where sheep graze freely. In the final section the road snakes its way up the escarpment of the Black Mountains and into the narrow slot between between Lord Hereford's Knob and Hay Bluff.

What follows is more than enough reward for the hard work of the climb: a 12 mile descent down the Vale of Ewyas, one of the most beautiful valleys in Wales, if not the world. Though it's possible to ride this section at speed, the road is narrow and rough in places, so it's sensible to take it easy. This is a ride to savour. The whole valley feels like a remote sanctuary hidden between the rolling farmland of Herefordshire and the bleak, windblown uplands of the Black Mountains. One of the first buildings on the way down is the tiny church at Capel-y-Ffin that sits within a circle of ancient yew trees. Nearby, 150 years ago, an Anglican mystic named Father Ignatius established a monastic community here. His vision was brutally ascetic and ultimately it was a doomed endeavour. In the 1920s a group of bohemian artists took the place of the monks, led by the artist, stonemason and writer Eric Gill who recalled how they "bathed naked in the pools... and smelled a world untouched by men of business".

START & FINISH: Hay-on-Wye • DISTANCE: 35 miles/56km • TOTAL ASCENT: 1018m
TERRAIN: Lanes. Challenging

Llanthony Abbey

Capel-y-Ffin

All very nice when the sun is shining, but the cold winters, the rain and the sheer isolation soon wore them down too and they fled to the rather less rugged landscape of the Chilterns.

Ignatius and Gill were following a path well trodden by the hermits, monks and mystics who have come here as far back as St David, who established a small monastic cell at Llanthony in the sixth century. Five hundred years later an Augustinian priory was built on the same site. Though one of the most remarkable buildings of medieval Wales, the monks at Llanthony also suffered from the vagaries of the landscape, the weather and also, according to Giraldus Cambrensis, the "barbarous people" who lived here. The priory entered a terminal decline and by the time Henry VIII delivered his *coup de grâce*, there were just a handful of monks living here.

Centuries later the ivy-clad ruins became a popular tourist destination to those of a Romantic sensibility. Among the visitors were the Wordsworths, who walked the length and breadth of the valley, and J.M.W. Turner, who painted the idyllic scene.

Beyond Llanthony, the route follows the River Honddu to its confluence with the River Monnow. Well worth a short detour is the village of Cwmyoy with its extraordinary church that leans in all directions. The route rounds the southern flank of Hatterall Hill, a dark wall that rises like an ocean swell above the gentle patchwork of western Herefordshire, and begins the return journey north up the Monnow Valley. These valleys are among the inspirations for Bruce Chatwin's celebrated borderlands novel *On the Black Hill*, Allen Ginsberg's *Wales Visitation* (he dropped LSD at Llanthony in 1967) and Owen Sheers' wartime fantasy *Resistance*.

It's a long, steadily uphill ride to the wide plateau of a pass a couple of miles beyond Craswall, and then a long descent down cool, damp Cusop Dingle back into Hay-on-Wye.

Download route info at thebikeshow.net/14BH

PUBS & PIT STOPS

LLANTHONY PRIORY HOTEL, Llanthony NP7 7NN (01873 890487) Cellar pub in the abbey ruins. Bar meals, B&B and camping.

TREATS, Llanthony, NP7 7NN (01873 890867) Café, bunkhouse and riverside camping.

SKIRRID MOUNTAIN INN, Llanvihangel Crucorney NP7 8DH (01873 890258) Macabre village inn.

THE BULL'S HEAD, Craswall HR2 0PN (01981 510616) Remote dining pub. Call ahead to check opening times and book.

THE BRIDGE, Michaelchurch Escley, HR2 0JW (01981 510646) Off the route but good food, riverside garden, upmarket B&B and camping.

BIKE SHOP: Drovers Cycles. Forest Rd, Hay-on-Wye HR3 5EH (01497 822419) Outstanding local bike shop. Bike hire available.

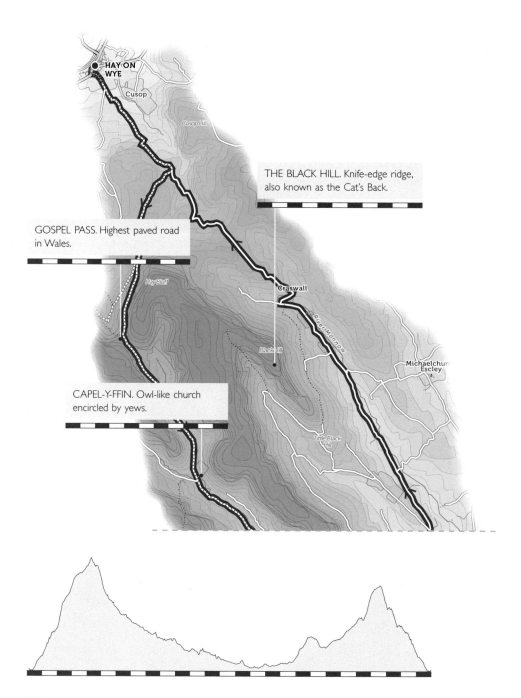

HAY ON WYE

Cusop

Cusop Hill

THE BLACK HILL. Knife-edge ridge, also known as the Cat's Back.

GOSPEL PASS. Highest paved road in Wales.

Hay Bluff

Craswall

River Monnow

Black Hill

Michaelchurch Escley

CAPEL-Y-FFIN. Owl-like church encircled by yews.

Little Black Hill

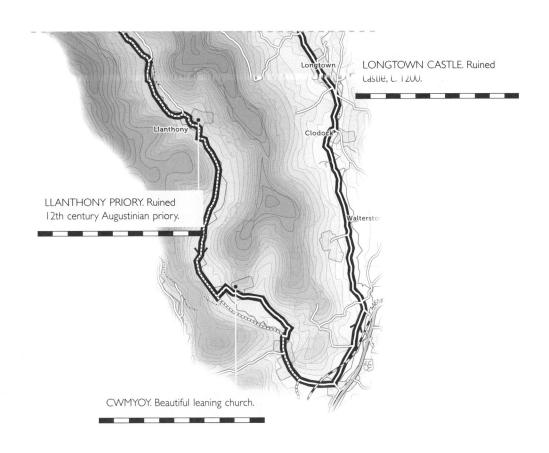

LONGTOWN CASTLE. Ruined castle, c. 1200.

LLANTHONY PRIORY. Ruined 12th century Augustinian priory.

CWMYOY. Beautiful leaning church.

Longtown castle

Cwmyoy church

No.15

USK VALLEY RAMBLE

Peel back the years of Welsh history in a pastoral ride to a perfect pub
up one of Wales's greatest rivers

———

More than any other ride in the book, this ride illustrates Wales's long history and gives food for thought about its future. In terms of physical geography it's a simple route up the River Usk, from its mouth at Newport to Clytha Park, some 25 meandering miles upstream. But in terms of human geography, it's a more complex story of change and adaptation.

At 73 miles long, the Usk is, after the Towy, the longest river that flows entirely within Wales. The ride begins by following National Cycle Route 88 through Newport's industrial armpit towards Caerleon. This inauspicious start makes the sudden appearance of a 6,000-seater Roman amphitheatre such a surprise. Known as Isca Augusta, Caerleon was a major Roman army fortress and there's plenty to explore here, both outdoors and in the town's museum. After crossing the bridge at Caerleon, the route leaves the urban world behind, and the change is dramatic as views open up across the Usk floodplain.

Spanning the river is a white-painted suspension bridge built for the Ryder Cup, which was held here in 2010 and bankrolled by huge taxpayer subsidies. The bridge is little used now since it's on the private land of the Celtic Manor golf resort, which was developed in the 1980s on the site of an old manor house that was, for much of the 20th

century, a maternity hospital. Sir Terry Matthews, the businessman who founded and still owns the Celtic Manor, was one of more than 60,000 babies born there. And I was another.

Overlooking the white bridge is a glitzy clubhouse and right next to it, quite visible from the lane, is a roofless, ramshackle farmhouse. It was saved from the bulldozers by Cadw, the national agency charged with preserving Wales's architectural patrimony, which in the Usk valley means rambling granges, hulking, slit-windowed barns, majestic stone bridges, tiny, exquisite churches, and, yes, small tumbledown farmhouses. In Welsh, Cadw means 'to keep' or 'to protect'. The 1970s brought a brand new dual carriageway and the 1980s a golf resort for the international jet set. Each has altered the atmosphere of the Usk valley forever. What remains, both its natural beauty and its many historic buildings, badly needs our protection.

The A449 has not only redefined the geography of the Usk valley, it has defaced its soundscape, and the route threads its way along old lanes as far as Usk. This was the original Roman legionary fortress in Wales until flooding forced a relocation downstream to Caerleon. It's a genteel town with narrow streets and more than its fair share of interesting buildings, from the Norman castle to

START & FINISH: Newport, Gwent • DISTANCE: 39 miles/62km • TOTAL ASCENT: 701m
TERRAIN: Lanes. Moderate

143

Llancayo

the Victorian prison with its pair of enormous and carefully trained wisteria. Housed in a cavernous barn, the volunteer-run Museum of Rural Life is a joyful treasure trove of mysterious household objects, terrifying agricultural equipment and brightly painted vintage tractors.

It's north out of Usk on the B4598 as far as the windmill at Llancayo. The most prominent landmark in this section of the valley, it was built during the Napoleonic Wars of the early 1800s by Edward Berry, a Yorkshire textiles merchant who had made a fortune and lost it gambling, then made it again. Tragically, his Huguenot wife was guillotined during the French Revolution and he retired to Monmouthshire to live the life of a gentleman farmer. At some point the five-storey windmill burned down and stood as a wreck until it was restored just a few years ago, and it's now a holiday home available to rent.

The road then heads up a stiff climb to Bettws Newydd, and gets even steeper up to Coed-y-Bwnydd, the largest and best-preserved Iron Age hill fort in Monmouthshire. It's wooded now and in late spring the undulating concentric ramparts are an ocean swell of iridescent bluebells with hot pink flecks of red campion and bright, white stitchwort. After the climbing it's a relief that the next section, to the Clytha Arms, is all downhill. This is my favourite pub in Wales and it really has it all: architecture, atmosphere, delicious local food, outstanding beer and cider, and a few bedrooms for overnight stays.

Though the peaks of the Black Mountains around Abergavenny beckon to the north, the return journey to Newport begins with a run through the landscaped grounds of Clytha Park. From Bettws Newydd you retrace your route all the way back through Usk until just past Llantrisant where a right turn heads over the River Usk at Newbridge. The ride back to Caerleon follows a magical lost lane on the western bank of the river through Glen Usk. Both Geoffrey of Monmouth and Chrétien de Troyes place Camelot, the fabled court of King Arthur, in Caerleon. As nobody knows for sure if King Arthur even existed, it's all conjecture, but the legend completes the Usk valley's just claim to be a microcosm of Welsh history.

Download route info at thebikeshow.net/15UV

PUBS & PIT STOPS

THE GREYHOUND INN, Llantrisant NP15 1LE (01291 672505) Large country inn.

NAG'S HEAD, 6 Twyn Square, Usk, NP15 1BH (01291 672820). Nice pub serving food.

CLYTHA ARMS, Clytha NP7 9BW (01873 840206) Relaxed rural pub, real ales, good food, B&B.

NEWBRIDGE INN, Newbridge-on-Usk NP15 1LY (01633 451000) Upmarket dining pub with riverside garden.

BIKE SHOP: South Wales Bikes, 45 Caerleon Road, Newport NP19 7BW (01633 243384)

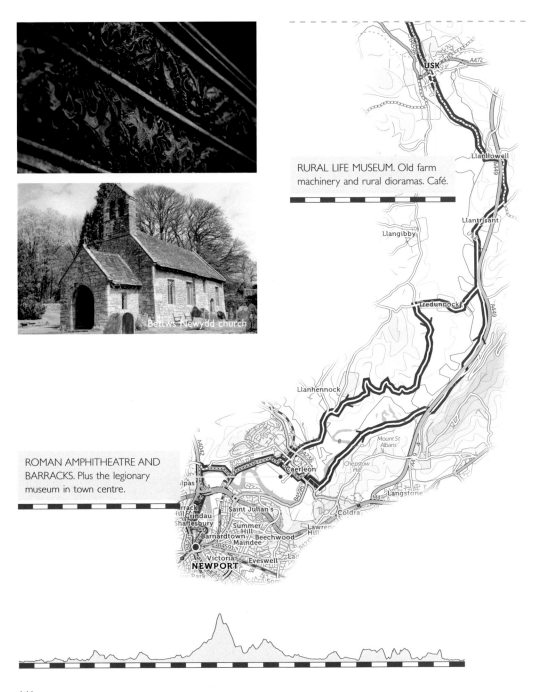

RURAL LIFE MUSEUM. Old farm machinery and rural dioramas. Café.

ROMAN AMPHITHEATRE AND BARRACKS. Plus the legionary museum in town centre.

Bettws Newydd church

WILD SWIMMING SPOT. Via the footpath on the south bank of Pant-y-Goitre bridge.

BETTWS NEWYDD. Church with rood screen and loft, ancient yew.

LANCAYO WINDMILL. Dates from the time of the Napoleonic Wars.

COED-Y-BWNYDD. Iron Age hill fort carpeted in spring bluebells.

Clytha Arms

No. 16

THREE PEAKS

A deceptively laid-back circuit Abergavenny,
Wales's self-proclaimed capital of cycling, with an optional sting in the tail

———

Every year since 1963, fleet-footed fell runners and hardy hill walkers have beaten a path to Abergavenny for the Three Peaks Trial, a mountain marathon to the tops of the Sugarloaf, the Skirrid and the Blorenge, the three hills that lend the town its somewhat alpine atmosphere. This ride takes in the same three peaks, although only summits of one of them, and there's even a bail-out option for those who dislike climbing.

Setting off from Abergavenny the road heads uphill past Maindiff Court, a country house where Adolph Hitler's deputy Rudolf Hess was held during the Second World War. Apparently he was a keen rambler and spent long hours exploring the area, at complete liberty from his captors. The first hill on the menu is the stark, shattered sandstone ridge of the Skirrid – the Holy Mountain, St Michael's Mount or, to give it its proper Welsh name, Ysgyryd Fawr. Legends abound: some say the mountain got its distinctive shape when it was rent in two at the moment of Christ's crucifixion; others that the devil caused the landslide by stamping his foot; or that it's Jack o'Kent's heel print from when he leaped across from the Sugarloaf. In medieval times people made pilgrimage here, and during the Reformation Catholics held clandestine masses in the ruined chapel on the summit. It's not possible to ride to the top, so the route skirts the hill's western flank before descending to cross the River Gavenny at Llanvihangel Crucorney and begin the climb towards the Sugarloaf.

The summit of the Sugarloaf is firmly mountain bike territory so this touring route is more of a circumnavigation. A miniature Fujiyama, the Sugarloaf is a good-looking mountain from any direction, but the view from the north is especially impressive in late summer, when its flanks are a purple haze of heather. There's an optional short but steep climb to Patrishow where a perfect little church, a hermit's grotto and holy well perch overlooking the valley of the Grwyne Fawr, one of the long streams that drain from the Black Mountains into the Usk.

Sometimes the best bike rides are not the ones that follow the most direct route from A to B, but those that take the long way around on the lanes less travelled. In this spirit, a scenic detour up the Grwyne Fechan is more than justified as it may be the loveliest little valley in the Black Mountains. The narrow lane winds up the valley and romantics will want to carry on up to the top to explore the ruin of a grand Georgian house known as the Hermitage. Its grandeur is quite out of place at the top of a remote Welsh valley. It's said to have been built by John Macnamara, a wealthy gambler and infamous libertine, to house his mistress in splendid isolation. The descent is through Llanbedr and Llangenny and halfway between the two villages is a secret swimming spot. It's off to the left of the lane – leave the bikes at the top and follow the public footpath down a steep, wooded bank and across a stone

START & FINISH: Abergavenny • DISTANCE: 38 miles/61km • TOTAL ASCENT: 1336m
TERRAIN: Lanes. Challenging

The Skirrid

packhorse bridge, then turn left to find a small beach beside the meadow. Beware, as even in high summer the water is bracing.

Past Llangenny, it's a fast descent to the A40 at Glangrwyney. The road to Gilwern crosses the Usk on a rickety box girder bridge that looks like it's been dropped in from a Bobbie Gentry lyric, and the derelict paper mill, half hidden in the trees on the banks of the Usk, adds to the Southern Gothic vibe.

After skirting around Gilwern, the route negotiates the Heads of the Valleys Road, the big physical barrier in this part of the Usk valley, taking a path beneath it. Climbing through Govilon the route crosses the disused Heads of the Valleys railway line and this is the bail-out point for anyone who doesn't fancy the leg-busting ascent of the third peak, the Blorenge mountain, that lies ahead. Just follow the railway path (National Cycle Route 46) to Llanfoist and Abergavenny. Else, continue up the lane, enjoying the ever expanding horizon on the climb out of the trees. In the world of cycling, the most famous climb on the Blorenge is the Tumble, up its northern face. This quiet, little known western ascent is known locally as the Tyla (pronounced Tiller).

On the way up, the narrow lane rounds Gilwern Hill, climbing high above the Clydach Gorge and through an eerie landscape of overgrown spoil heaps from the ironworks that once devoured the hillside. The road passes through the remains of Pwll Du, a village of mineworkers and quarrymen that was abandoned in 1963, its residents moved down the hill to Govilon. Beneath the surface is the Ogof Draenen, at 41 miles the second longest cave system in Britain and a magnet to potholers. Across the B4246 the road rises to crest the mountain by a pair of radio transmitters, from where it's a long, eye-watering descent down the eastern side of the mountain, through beech woods and farmland to Llanfoist and back to Abergavenny.

Download route info at thebikeshow.net/16TP

PUBS & PIT STOPS

THE SKIRRID INN, Llanvihangel Crucorney, NP7 8DH. 01873 890258. Among the oldest pubs in Wales, with a grim history. Rumours of ghosts.

THE DRAGON'S HEAD, Llangenny, NP8 1HD. 01873 810350. Friendly village pub with good, simple food including curry served the Welsh way with 'half and half' rice and chips. Small campsite by the river.

THE BELL, Glangrwyney, NP8 1EH. 01873 811115. Stonebuilt pub on the main A40 road. Sunday roasts, and rooms available for overnight stays.

LAMB AND FOX INN, Pwll Ddu, NP4 9SS. 07790 682832. Low-ceiling old miners' and quarrymen's pub. Beer from the local Rhymney Brewery, pub grub, wood fires.

MIDDLE NINFA FARM, NP7 9LE. 01873 85466. Tiny, secluded campsite with great views set in 23 acres of woodland, orchards and garden. Also has bunkhouse.

THE KINGS ARMS, Abergavenny, NP7 5AA. 01873 855074. Relaxed pub serving good food.

THE ANGEL HOTEL, NP7 5EN. Abergavenny, 01873 857121 Grand hotel with a refined, arty vibe and famous afternoon teas.

BIKE SHOPS: Gateway Cycles, 5 Brecon Road, Abergavenny, NP7 5UH. 01873 858519. M&D Cycles, 36 Frogmore Street, Abergavenny, NP7 5AN. 01873 854980.

BIKE HIRE: Hopyard Cycles, Govilon, NP7 9SE. 01873 830219.

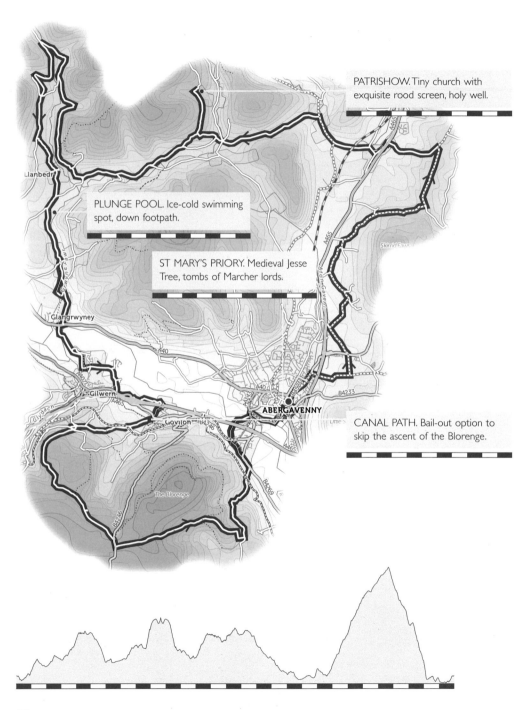

PATRISHOW. Tiny church with exquisite rood screen, holy well.

PLUNGE POOL. Ice-cold swimming spot, down footpath.

ST MARY'S PRIORY. Medieval Jesse Tree, tombs of Marcher lords.

CANAL PATH. Bail-out option to skip the ascent of the Blorenge.

The Sugarloaf

The Tyla

IRON MOUNTAIN

A ride through South Wales's industrial history on
traffic-free railway and canal paths

———

While riding up the old railway line that steadily climbs the steep-sided valley of the Afon Clwyd, take a look down at your bicycle. From its sparkling spokes to its slinky chain, the bike is a crowning achievement of a technology that is a shorthand for human progress. Iron is the recurrent theme on this grand and mostly traffic-free circumnavigation of the Blorenge mountain, the towering full stop at the eastern end of the South Wales coalfield.

Mankind's earliest iron objects were made from iron that came from meteorites. Around 3,000 years ago people discovered that if they heated certain kinds of rock hot enough, iron would flow out of them. Going from primitive cast iron, brittle and full of impurities, to a mass-produced material that's strong and workable is the story of steel. A key chapter of that story was played out in this hilly, remote and sparsely populated corner of south-east Wales. Beneath the rough, russet moorland lie rich deposits of iron ore, lime and coal: the three ingredients that supercharged the iron production technologies of the industrial revolution.

This ride makes full use of the network of canals and disused railway lines built for the iron industry. They were built by hand with picks and shovels by unnamed thousands of labourers. It's

thanks to their back-breaking toil that we have some fine routes for cycling, walking and boating that make light work of the hilly terrain.

Starting in Pontypool, the route follows National Cycle Route 492 up the valley of the Afon Lwyd. The first town after Pontypool is Abersychan. It's a coal town and the birthplace of Roy Jenkins, the politician, historian and great reforming Home Secretary of the 1960s, who presided over abolishing capital punishment, decriminalising homosexuality, relaxing censorship, reforming divorce law and legalising abortion. In 1987, Jenkins, the son of a miner, was elevated to the House of Lords and elected Chancellor of Oxford University.

A forge is where the brittle pig iron straight from the furnace is heated, refined and worked into shape. The work was extremely dangerous and required skill, huge strength and the ability to endure searing temperatures. The first forge for the iron made in the furnaces at Blaenavon was at Cwmavon across the valley, but quite visible from the railway path is a neat whitewashed terrace of ironworkers' cottages, the best preserved example of traditional workers' terraced housing anywhere in the South Wales valleys.

Though the very first ironworks in the valley used charcoal to melt the iron ore, switching to

---

START & FINISH: Pontypool • DISTANCE: 31 miles/50km • TOTAL ASCENT: 715m
TERRAIN: Cycle tracks, canal towpath and lanes. Challenging.

Big Pit

Cwmavon

Big Pit

coal, mined in the valley, meant production could be dramatically increased. At peak production there were 160 drift mines (tunnels dug horizontally) and 30 deep mines (shafts sunk vertically) in the area. Big Pit, as the name suggests, was the biggest, employing 1,400 men in the 1920s. The coal here is high-grade 'steam coal' and was in heavy demand from steam vessels at sea. As the 20th century wore on, a lack of investment in mechanisation, global competition and the switch to oil and gas saw British coal mines begin a long decline and Big Pit closed in 1980. It now hosts the National Coal Museum, one of Wales's nine national museums and perhaps the best. All the museum guides are former mineworkers and visitors get the chance to go underground and see much of the mine just as it was left when it closed.

From Blaenavon, the railway line path continues over the top towards Brynmawr. The surface is of variable quality (hopefully it will be upgraded throughout before too long) and the B4248 offers a smoother alternative for those prepared to brave the motor traffic. The cycle path skirts the edge of Brynmawr and makes a long, gentle descent into the Clydach Gorge, where more disused industrial buildings sit silent among the ancient broadleaf woodland – the gorge was too steep for the wood to be felled. From the railway path there are fine views north across the Usk valley to the peaks of the Black Mountains, a glimpse of another Wales beyond the Valleys.

Follow the railway path until the wharf at Govilon, where the route switches onto the towpath of the 'Mon and Brec' canal, one of the jewels of the British canal network. The canal clings to the side of the Blorenge mountain and passes through more ancient beech woods above the village of Llanfoist. If time is running out, it's possible to take the train back from Abergavenny to Pontypool – the station is a pleasant two-mile ride from Llanfoist across Abergavenny's castle meadows. Otherwise, simply carry on along the canal towpath as it winds its way around the eastern flank of the Blorenge and down the Usk valley for the 11 miles back to Pontypool.

Download route info at thebikeshow.net/17IM

PUBS & PIT STOPS

MINERS' CANTEEN, Big Pit, Blaenafon, Torfaen NP4 9XP (02920 573650). The original mine canteen.

THE WHISTLE INN, Blaenavon NP4 9SJ (01495 790403). Pub by the steam railway, basic campsite.

TAFARN Y BONT. Church Lane, Govilon NP7 9RP (01873 830720) Canalside pub.

GOYTRE WHARF CAFÉ, Llanover NP7 9EW (01873 880899) Café among old canal wharf buildings and woodland.

HORSESHOE INN. Old Abergavenny Road, Mamhilad (01873 880542) Just off the canal. Fine views, pub grub.

BIKE HIRE: Hopyard Cycles, Govilon NP7 9SE (01873 830219)

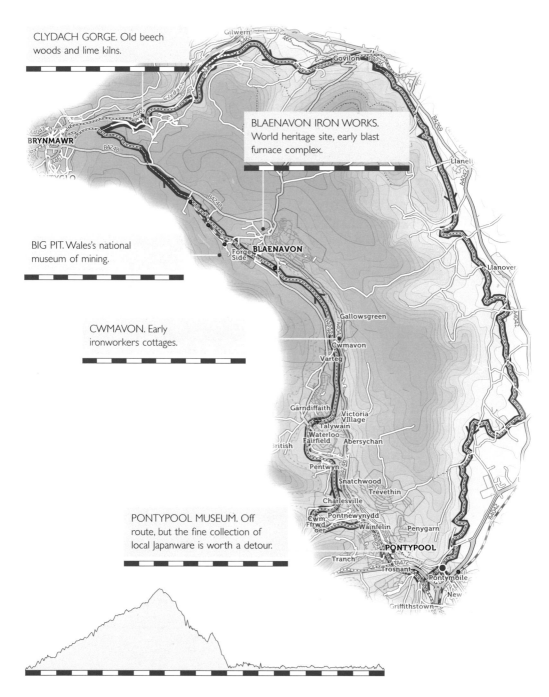

CLYDACH GORGE. Old beech woods and lime kilns.

BLAENAVON IRON WORKS. World heritage site, early blast furnace complex.

BIG PIT. Wales's national museum of mining.

CWMAVON. Early ironworkers cottages.

PONTYPOOL MUSEUM. Off route, but the fine collection of local Japanware is worth a detour.

WELCOME TO THE VALLEYS

A ride on the wild mountain roads high above the coal and steel
heartland of South Wales

―――

As an upland metropolis, the South Wales valleys are unique in Britain. Scarcely inhabited until the mid-18th century, first came the ironworks, then the coal mines. As people flocked to the Valleys in search of work, long, thin settlements were packed into the deep gashes in the mountainous terrain. Once the industrial heartland of Wales, most of the work that brought people here is long gone. Yet the Valleys are still home to a third of the population of Wales. A recent report for the Welsh Government described the Valleys as "a distressed area unique in Great Britain for the depth and concentration of its problems". Yet still people remain here, perhaps because of the strong communities that grew up around the heavy industries, perhaps because they see no way out.

Though many disused railway lines have been converted into cycling and walking paths, they can make for monotonous riding. Yet where there are valleys there are – by definition – hills. It's up here, among the clouds, where the best cycling is to be found. There are some superlative views and this ride, taking in both hills and valleys, gives a sense of the profound change that's been wrought by two and a half centuries of rapid development and slow decline.

Starting deep in the Rhymney valley, the ride begins with a short section along the riverside cycle path in Bargoed, then the first challenge is the climb up Commin Road onto the ridge road north. It's a road that becomes increasingly spectacular, with views down to the tightly packed terraced streets of New Tredegar, a town built for workers in a half dozen collieries in the valley, all long since closed.

The aerial view gives a good impression of the sheer density of the Valleys' towns. The neat terraces were a vast improvement on the hovels of the early years, which were built cheaply to house a workforce that was considered as more or less disposable. Families of ten or more often occupied cramped rooms with dirt floors that were continually damp. There were no toilets so buckets were emptied into the gullies in the streets, and the foul water flooded homes after heavy rain.

It's no surprise that the global cholera epidemics of the 19th century hit the Valleys especially hard. A little further on, as the mountain road descends towards Tredegar, stands the remains of the town's cholera cemetery. Gravestones, chipped and crooked and overgrown with grasses, stand as a forlorn reminder of the many hundreds who died in the outbreaks of the early and mid-1800s. People had no idea where cholera came from or how to cure it, and the fear and sadness that swept the population fed into the religious revivals of the time, as church and chapel bells tolled for the dead.

START & FINISH: Bargoed • DISTANCE: 26 miles/41km • TOTAL ASCENT: 805m
TERRAIN: Lanes and some gravel mountain roads. Challenging

Tredegar

Turning west, the route descends into Rhymney, the coal mining town whose 'sad bells' were made famous in a song by Pete Seeger that was a massive hit for 1960s psychedelic folk-rockers, The Byrds. The lyrics were taken from *Gwalia Deserta* by Rhymney-born miner-turned-poet, Idris Davies. Continuing all the way through Rhymney, the route threads its way east along the cycle path through Parc Bryn Bach. Built on the site of an open cast coal mine, it's one of many examples of industrial land turned over to leisure and recreation. It was once a very different place. One contemporary observer described it so: "Utterly remote at the head of the Sirhowy valley, the town was a man-made hell. Men and children worked killing hours in the smoke and filth of the foundries and were maimed by molten metal."

Negotiating the streets of Tredegar, you'll pass through the Circle, where stands, facing the famous clock tower, a statue of Aneurin 'Nye' Bevan. A Labour politician, Bevan was the architect of the National Health Service, a system of public healthcare he modelled on the Tredegar Workmen's Medical Aid Society, promising to the British people, "We are going to 'Tredegar-ise' you." A couple of miles further on is the windswept hillside where Bevan would hold massed, open-air meetings and there is now a memorial to Tredegar's favourite son.

From the Bevan memorial the journey south is on the rough mountain road along Cefn Manmoel, a broad ridge that separates Tredegar from Ebbw Vale. At the southern end it's a steep descent back into the Sirhowy valley and up the other side to the church of St Sannan at Bedwellty. The hilltop church is 13th century but the site is almost certainly older – there's a holy well nearby, which is often a clue to ancient Celtic and pre-Christian sacred sites. With fine sight lines it may once have been used to relay messages from the Brecon Beacons in the north to Caerphilly in the south. After a final farewell to the mountains it's time to begin the descent back to Bargoed.

Download route info at thebikeshow.net/18WV

PUBS & PIT STOPS

MOUNTAIN ASH INN, Tredegar NP22 5BQ (01495 724592) Just off route, mountain pub, food served.

THE FARMERS' ARMS, Brewery Row, Rhymney NP22 5EZ (01685 8402570) Historic Valleys pub.

WINDSOR ARMS, Bute Town NP22 5QJ (01685 841093) Ironworkers' pub in historic model village.

THE OLYMPIA, Morgan Street, Tredegar NP22 3ND (01495 712910) Cavernous Wetherspoons' in an old cinema. All day food.

BIKE HIRE: Parc Bryn Bach, Merthyr Road, Tredegar NP22 3AY (01495 355920)

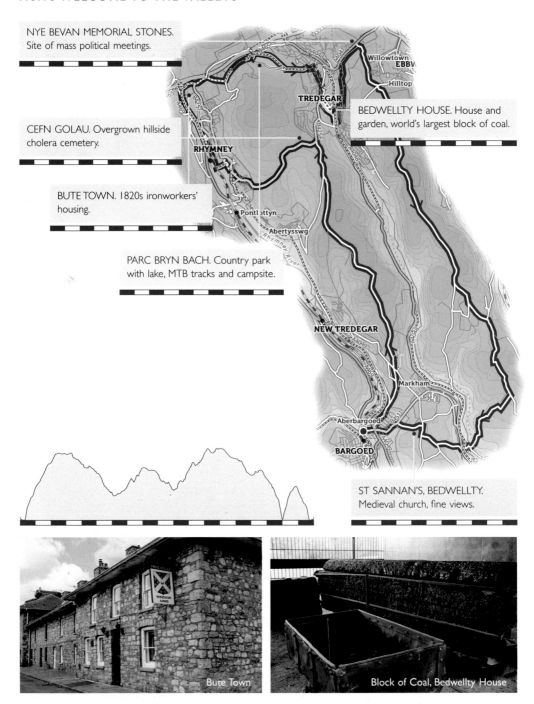

NYE BEVAN MEMORIAL STONES. Site of mass political meetings.

CEFN GOLAU. Overgrown hillside cholera cemetery.

BUTE TOWN. 1820s ironworkers' housing.

PARC BRYN BACH. Country park with lake, MTB tracks and campsite.

BEDWELLTY HOUSE. House and garden, world's largest block of coal.

ST SANNAN'S, BEDWELLTY. Medieval church, fine views.

Bute Town

Block of Coal, Bedwellty House

Cefn Golau cholera cemetery

SEASIDE SEDUCTION

Easy, traffic free riding on Llanelli's miraculously transformed post industrial coastline

---

Let's face it, we all have friends and family who don't ride bikes. To tempt them to give cycling a try, what's needed is a special kind of ride. One that's pancake flat and traffic free, with amazing scenery and plenty to see and do along the way. This ride, on Wales's south coast around Llanelli, is the perfect instrument of seduction for the hesitant cyclist.

The Millennium Coastal Park extends on the northern shore of the Loughor estuary either side of the town of Llanelli all the way to Pembrey Burrows. Much of this coastline was once home to the steel and tin plate works that earned 19th century Llanelli the nickname of Tinopolis. The decline of these industries in the 1970s left a 2,000-acre expanse of polluted, post-industrial wasteland, and so its transformation into green coastal parkland is nothing short of astonishing. Though the area attracts more than a million visitors a year, it rarely feels overcrowded.

The icing on the cake is the wide, deliciously smooth, traffic-free cycle track that reminds us just how good a cycle path can be and, sadly, just how off-putting are Britain's countless miles of 'crap cycle lanes'. The huge numbers of people who use the cycle track, either as a route to and from work or simply to get out and about in the fresh air, should leave our politicians and transport planners in no doubt that when it comes to high-quality cycle infrastructure, if you build it, they will come.

This is a linear, out and back route that starts at Gowerton train station, though if arriving by car it's also possible to start at Llanelli Wetlands Centre, where there's plentiful free parking. The ride hugs the coast west all the way to Kidwelly, with its imposing Norman castle. The route can be ridden in either direction, or if you need to hire bikes then it will be necessary to start in the middle at Burry Port, where the bike hire shop is, and head one way before looping back to complete the circuit. The full distance there and back is 41 miles, too far for young children or anyone not used to spending a whole day in the saddle. Fortunately, the railway line between Gowerton and Llanelli offers a useful bail-out option. Alternatively, you can keep it simple by just deciding to turn back when the time is right.

From Gowerton, you'll quickly pick up National Cycle Route 4 heading west across the River Loughor and along the edge of the Llanelli Wetland Centre, a 450-acre mosaic of lakes, pools, streams and lagoons adjoining the salt marshes and seashore. There are fine sea views across the Loughor estuary to the hills of the Gower Peninsula and birdwatchers will want to look out for the huge variety of species – some quite rare – that gather here.

The route brushes the edge of Llanelli and passes the old dock, built for exporting coal and tin plate but now redeveloped as a waterside resi-

---

START & FINISH: Gowerton • DISTANCE: 22 miles/35km • TOTAL ASCENT: 120m
TERRAIN: Mostly surfaced cycle track, some unsurfaced and lanes. Easy

dential, business and leisure district. Eventually the sports fields and lawns give way to a wilder-feeling landscape leading to the spectacular earth sculpture 'Walking with the Sea Turning with the Sea', designed by the artist Richard Harris and built with 115,000 cubic metres of pulverised fuel ash from a nearby power station. Harris, a lifelong surfer, says the earthwork evokes "a wave travelling towards a waiting shore… a coming together of the relationship between land, sea and people".

Burry Port is a former industrial town with a horseshoe-shaped harbour and new yachting marina. The most celebrated visitor was Amelia Earhart, the record-breaking American aviatrix, who landed here in 1928 as the first woman to fly the Atlantic, though she didn't actually pilot the plane. "I was just baggage, like a sack of potatoes," she said, "Maybe someday I'll try it alone." In 1932 she did, and the rest is history.

West of Burry Port lies Pembrey Burrows, a windblown landscape of Corsican pine and tufty sand dunes. It leads to the sands of Cefn Sidan beach, at eight miles one of Wales's longest. This is the scene of the annual Battle of the Beach, the UK's only beach bike race that sees mountain bikers, cyclo-crossers, gravel racers and fat bike fanatics cut it up on the vast expanse of sand. The route heads on along a combination of unsurfaced cycle paths and quiet lanes as far as Kidwelly.

Now some way from the sea, Kidwelly was once a key military stronghold for the Anglo-Norman kings of England during their battles with the Welsh princes. Hundreds of years later it was a coal port during Wales's industrial heyday. It's now turned its back on the sea and the dock was used as a municipal waste dump. The fine castle remains, perched high above the River Gwendraeth. From Kidwelly it's either a 20-minute train journey back to Gowerton (the train also stops at Llanelli and Burry Port), or you can simply turn around and ride back, with the prevailing westerly wind blowing you along like a dream.

Download route info at thebikeshow.net/19SS

PUBS & PIT STOPS

SOSBAN, North Dock, Llanelli SA15 2LF (01554 270020) Chic dockside dining from top chefs Sian Rees and Ian Wood.

THE LIGHTHOUSE CAFÉ, The Harbour, Burry Port SA16 0ER (07817 945482) Overlooks the harbour where pioneering aviatrix Amelia Earhart once landed.

THE GATEHOUSE, 2 Castle Street, Kidwelly, SA17 5AX. (01554 891278) Small, cheery café with a sunny garden.

KIDWELLY BED & BREAKFAST, 62 Causeway Street, Kidwelly SA17 4SU. (01554 890716) Smart B&B.

BIKE SHOP: Llanelli & Burry Port Cycles, 47 Station Road, Burry Port SA16 0LP (01554 835895) Hire bikes available.

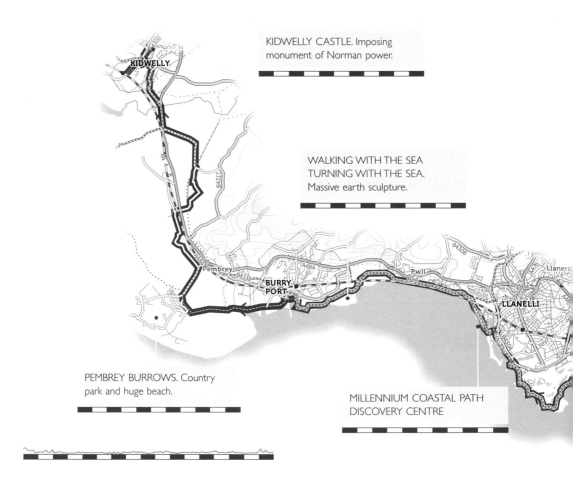

KIDWELLY CASTLE. Imposing
monument of Norman power.

WALKING WITH THE SEA
TURNING WITH THE SEA.
Massive earth sculpture.

PEMBREY BURROWS. Country
park and huge beach.

MILLENNIUM COASTAL PATH
DISCOVERY CENTRE

Walking with the Sea Turning with the Sea

WETLANDS CENTRE. 450 acres
of pools, marshes and lagoons.

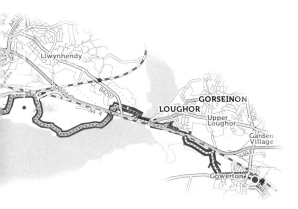

Kidwelly Castle

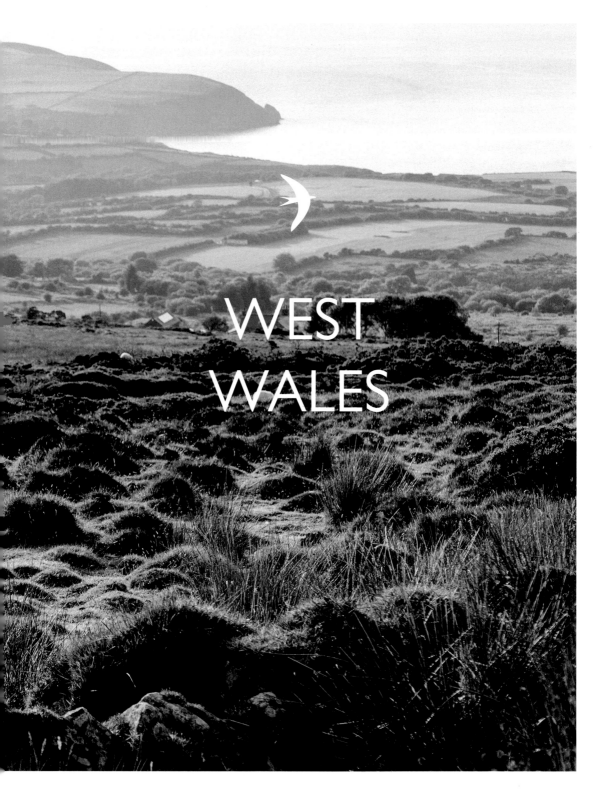

WEST
WALES

No.20

ONLY THE STONES REMAIN

A circuit of the enchanted landscape of North Pembrokeshire's Preseli massif
is a journey back to the Bronze Age

———

Nigel Tufnel, lead guitarist in the fictional heavy metal band Spinal Tap, said of the Bronze Age druids of Stonehenge, "No one knows who they were or what they were doing". Nor do we know how several dozen massive bluestones were moved from the Preseli Hills in west Wales to Salisbury Plain in Wiltshire. Most archaeologists think the huge stones were transported by sea, on rafts along the south coast of Wales, across the Bristol Channel and then up rivers and overland to Stonehenge. It would have been an astonishing undertaking, given the technologies of the time. Recent research suggests the stones weren't moved by people at all, but by glacial action more than half a million years ago, slowly dragging them from west Wales to Wiltshire.

However the stones got from here to there, what's beyond doubt is that for prehistoric Britons both the Preseli Hills and Salisbury Plain were very special places. Both landscapes are studded with standing stones, cairns, burial mounds and other ritual sites. Some archaeologists believe it was the landscape itself that was sacred and individual sites were merely focal points. To travel by bicycle is to travel at the speed of the land. This makes it the perfect way to appreciate a landscape as a single entity, perhaps in the way that our Bronze Age ancestors did. This ride leaves the coast behind and heads inland for a loop around Mynydd Preseli.

The cheerful harbour town of Fishguard sits at the mouth of the Afon Gwaun and the ride begins by following the river upstream, initially on the B4313 before crossing onto a narrow lane that traces its way up the valley. The Gwaun valley sets the pulse of geologists racing because it's a rare example of an ice-age meltwater channel: a valley scoured out by torrents that flowed as the glaciers retreated at the end of the last ice age. It's now densely forested with beech, hazel, ash and oak, and dotted with megalithic standing stones. In St Brynach's Church in Pontfaen there are two carved stone crosses from the Age of Saints and on the hillside north of Llanychaer there's a holy well to seek out. The whole place has an enchanted, timeless feel to it, as if the 20th century never arrived, save for a few cars and tractors.

It seems the locals haven't fully accepted the Gregorian calendar adopted by the rest of Britain in 1752; they still celebrate New Year's Day according to the older Julian calendar, currently on 13 January. On that day many children skip school to tour the homes in the valley, singing songs.

The route picks its way around the northern slopes of the Preselis on a network of quiet,

---

START & FINISH: Fishguard • DISTANCE: 39 miles/63km • TOTAL ASCENT: 1082m
TERRAIN: Lanes. Challenging

Mynachlog-ddu

narrow lanes. It's not always by the most direct route, but it's idyllic cycling country and the miles tick away easily. Leaving the Gwaun behind, it's on to the valley of the Afon Nyfer, climbing gradually to the village of Crymych. Along this section of the ride the dividing line between arable farmland and the rocky uplands is clear to see and soon enough, rounding the eastern end of the massif, the landscape becomes more rugged and exposed.

The sparse village of Mynachlog-ddu is best known as the home of the poet Waldo Williams. In 1946 he wrote a poem entitled Preseli, a passionate protest against the threat that the hills would be turned into a military training ground. It is not unheard of for stone circles and other prehistoric sites to be used as target practice by trigger-happy squaddies.

The last two lines are among the most quoted in all Welsh language poetry, in Williams' own English translation: "Hark! A roar and ravage through a windowless forest. To the wall! We must keep our well clear of this beast's dirt." Powerful stuff.

In the village is a collection of standing stones, several of which were helicoptered down from the summit ridge above the village. The lane then snakes its way along the contours of the southern edge of the massif, offering some stunning vistas south across Pembrokeshire's rolling farmland interior. Antiquarians will find this section slow going because there's a profusion of Bronze Age sites to investigate.

It's then a rollercoaster ride through Bernard's Well and Henry's Moat, rounding the whale-backed Mynydd Castlebythe. The final climb is just after Puncheston, up the slopes of Mynydd Cilciffeth. The reward is a five-star view out to sea and into the setting sun. It's then a swooping descent into the Gwaun valley and the return ride, retracing the outbound route from earlier in the day, along the B4313 back to Fishguard.

Download route info at thebikeshow.net/20OS

PUBS & PIT STOPS

DYFFRYN ARMS, Pontfaen SA65 9SG (01348 881305) Historic front room pub.

CRYMYCH ARMS, Crymych SA41 3RJ (01239 831435) Village pub opposite fish and chip shop.

TAFARN SINC, Rosebush SA66 7QU (01437 532214) Quirky, historic railway pub serving traditional Welsh food.

DROVERS' ARMS, Puncheston SA62 5RJ (01348 881469) Friendly local pub.

THE SHIP INN, 3 Newport Road, Fishguard SA65 9ND (01348 874033) Lower town pub crammed with photos and nicknacks.

FISHGUARD ARMS, 24 Main Street, Fishguard (01348 872763) One of the oldest buildings in Pembrokeshire.

THE GOURMET PIG, 32 West Street, Fishguard SA65 9AD (01348 874404). Quality café and deli.

GWAUN VALLEY BREWERY, Kilkiffeth Farm, Pontfaen SA65 9TP (01348 881304) Microbrewery, tiny campsite and holiday cottage.

THE MANOR TOWN HOUSE, 11 Main Street, Fishguard SA65 9HG (01348 873260) Small, elegant guesthouse with panoramic views.

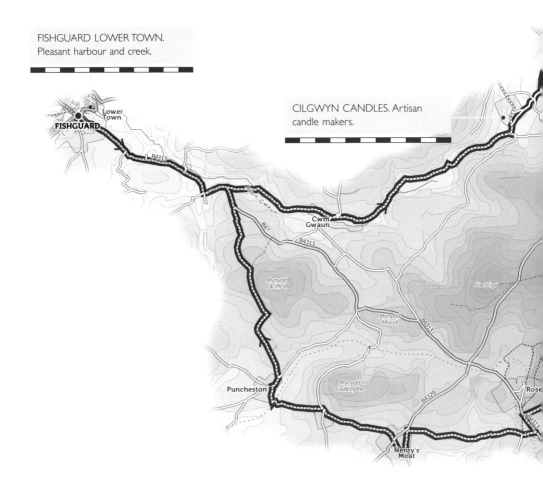

FISHGUARD LOWER TOWN.
Pleasant harbour and creek.

CILGWYN CANDLES. Artisan
candle makers.

Fishguard

The Dyffryn Arms

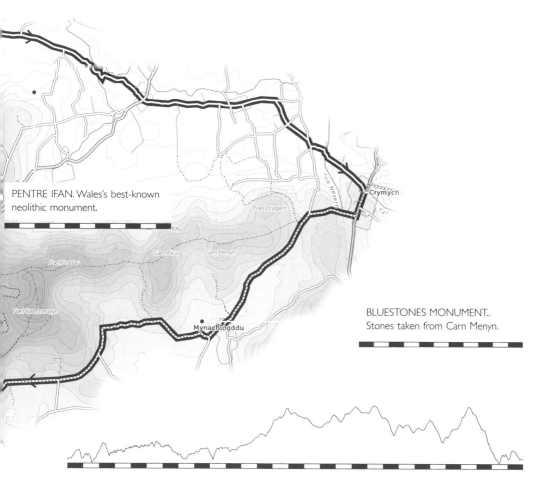

PENTRE IFAN. Wales's best-known neolithic monument.

Crymych

Foel Drygarn

Carn Bica

Carn Menyn

Foel Feddau

Foel Cwmcerwyn

Mynachlogddu

BLUESTONES MONUMENT.. Stones taken from Carn Menyn.

CELTIC COAST

A Pembrokeshire odyssey from Wales's ancient cathedral city
to the rocky shore of Strumble Head

———

In Britain a city is defined as a town containing a cathedral. This makes St Davids, with a population of just 1,600, by far the smallest city in Britain. Though small in size, it looms large in the history of Wales. The centuries after the Romans left is known as the 'age of saints', a time when missionaries travelled the Celtic world (Wales, Brittany, Cornwall and Ireland) spreading Christianity to people who mostly still held pagan beliefs. Born in west Wales, St David founded 12 monasteries. Despite his aristocratic birth he was an ascetic and he required monks to plough, plant and tend crops without using animals; monks were to drink only water and eat only bread with salt and herbs; they were to renounce all personal possessions and, when not doing physical labour, spend their time in prayer or reading and writing.

It must have made for a hard life, though very much in tune with the rugged, windblown landscape of this most westerly corner of Wales. If there is such a thing as a Celtic landscape (and surely there is, from Santiago de Compostela right up to the Western Isles) then the north coast of Pembrokeshire is its archetype: a farmland interior, studded with rocky outcrops, that ends abruptly with steep cliffs of dark, volcanic rock. Every so often a fast-flowing stream plunges to the sea down a deep, lush ravine and crashing

waves build up a fine sandy beach between towering headlands.

This ride begins out of St Davids on the A487 towards Solva, soon turning off the main road onto back lanes past a disused Second World War airfield that's now a nature reserve. Solva is a pretty village nestling in a narrow, pebbled inlet which, in geological terms, is a relatively newcomer, formed by meltwater at the end of the last ice age.

The next section is a traverse of the Pembrokeshire interior initially following the River Solva inland. This is potato country and the Pembrokeshire Early – a delicately skinned new potato with a nutty flavour – recently joined Champagne, Parma ham and Melton Mowbray pork pies as geographically distinctive foods protected by European law. At harvest time big trailers carry the potatoes from field to farm and, bumping their way along the narrow lanes, they always drop a few out the back. I reckon it's finders keepers and I've had no trouble filling a pannier with the tasty tubers.

Just after Castlemorris the route crosses the Corsydd Llangloffan nature reserve, in the headwaters of the Cleddau Rivers, and exceptionally rich in both flora and fauna. Eventually the pastoral landscape gives way to more rugged coastal terrain. Up ahead rises a ridge

---

START & FINISH: St Davids • DISTANCE: 41 miles/66km • TOTAL ASCENT: 901m
TERRAIN: Lanes. Challenging

Solva

Strumble Head

crowned at its western end by the Garn Fawr hill fort. Though the road skirts to the side of the summit it's still quite a climb.

At the top you can see all the way to Strumble Head. This was the scene of the last ever invasion of Britain when, in 1797, the French army landed with a ragtag force of 1,400 men, including a lot of recently released convicts. They had banked on the oppressed Welsh joining them in the march on London, but it soon descended into farce as the invaders surrendered to the local militia after two days of chaotic drunken looting. From the lighthouse at Strumble Head, you can see seals bobbing in the water or lounging on the rocks. The eagle-eyed may also spot porpoises out at sea.

This is a ride of two halves and the return leg to St David's is perhaps the most glorious coastal route in Wales. It's all quiet lanes, occasionally dipping down to sea level, but there's no serious climbing to do.

The sunny, salty, quayside village of Porthgain is well worth the short detour and there are good swimming beaches at Abereiddy. The coastal road rolls along happily for mile after mile, until it arrives by an entirely unexpected back-door route right at the door of the Bishop's Palace in St Davids. The palace, which stands in ruins beside the cathedral, looks as though it was once fabulously grand. Somewhere along the line St David's wealthy and powerful medieval successors must have set aside the plain and simple life for which Wales's patron saint is revered.

Download route info at thebikeshow.net/21CC

PUBS & PIT STOPS

THE SOUND CAFE, 18 High Street, St Davids SA62 6SD (01437 721717) Great breakfasts in this surfer hangout.

LAVENDER CAFÉ, The Old Chapel, Main St, Solva SA62 6UU (01437 721907) Arty café.

CAFÉ AT MELIN TREGWYNT, Castlemorris SA62 5UX (01348 891225) Little café serving good Welsh fare.

THE SHIP INN, Trefin SA62 5AX (01348 831445) 200-year-old village pub, food served.

THE SHED, Porthgain SA62 5BN (01348 831518) Quayside seafood café.

THE SLOOP INN, Porthgain SA62 5BN (01348 831449) Seaside pub with a sunny terrace.

CWTCH, 22 High Street, St Davids SA62 6SD (01437 720491) Award-winning bistro.

CAMPING WILD WALES, Trefin SA62 5AL (01348 837892) Campsite with a back to nature vibe.

CYCLE HIRE: TYF, 1 High Street, St Davids SA62 6SA (01437 720488)

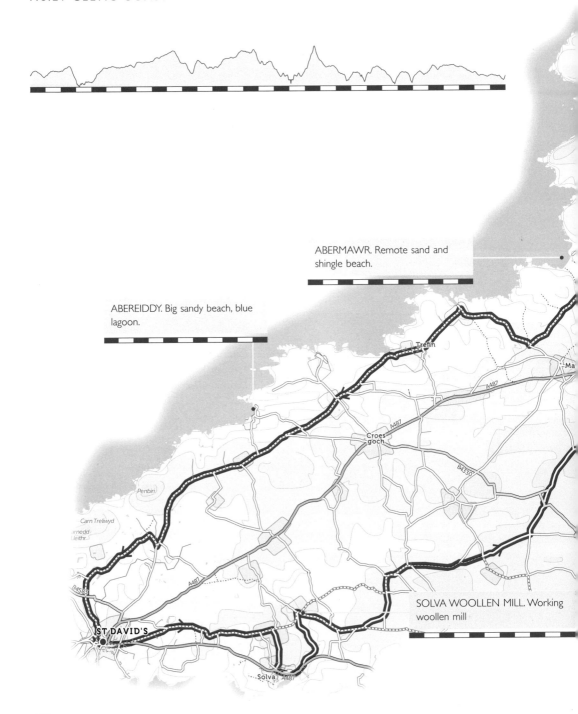

ABERMAWR. Remote sand and shingle beach.

ABEREIDDY. Big sandy beach, blue lagoon.

SOLVA WOOLLEN MILL. Working woollen mill

Trefin

Ma

A487

A487

Croes goch

B4330

Penbiri

Carn Treliwyd

rnedd leithr

B4583

A487

ST DAVID'S

Solva A487

STRUMBLE HEAD. Lighthouse, seal and porpoise spotting.

MELIN TREGWYNT. Working woollen mill, café.

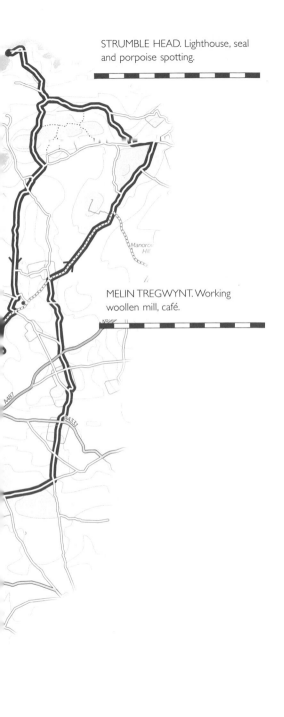

Melin Tregwynt

Aberbach

CLIFF AND CASTLE

From Norman might to hermit's hideaway via the sandy beaches and towering sea stacks of the Pembrokeshire coast

——

A few years ago, the Welsh Government proudly announced that Wales had become the first country in the world to have a continuous footpath along its entire coastline. The Pembrokeshire Coast Path – all 186 crinkly miles of it – is the jewel in the crown. Along the way are limestone cliffs, craggy volcanic headlands, sheltered fishing harbours and sandy beaches that wouldn't look out of place in the Caribbean. It's the best place for wild flowers in Wales and there's a wealth of birdlife too. The whole area is dotted with the remnants of millennia of human habitation, from megalithic standing stones and burial mounds to Norman castles and hermit hideaways. Unfortunately, almost all of the coast path is closed to cyclists, which is perfectly understandable as the path is often narrow and steep with precipitous drops. This ride takes in the longest section of the coast path that is open to bikes, between Stack Rocks and St Govan's Head.

Pembrokeshire feels a long way from anywhere but, back in the days when travelling by sea was faster than travelling by land, it was very much at the centre of things, thanks to its strategic position in the Irish Sea, sometimes known as the Celtic Mediterranean. The Vikings were frequent visitors – as raiders and traders but also as settlers – and many Pembro-

keshire place names have Scandinavian origins: Carew, Stackpole, Angle, Dale, Nash.

The early Norman kings of England left most of Wales to its own devices, but they made sure to control the coastal corridor from the Severn Sea to the ports of Pembrokeshire as a launchpad for their conquest and colonisation of Ireland. This ride begins in the town of Pembroke where, in 1093, Roger of Montgomery built a castle on a rocky promontory by the Cleddau Estuary. It's hard to think of a more imposing statement of Norman power. From its huge, round keep and crenellated battlements to its stone walls, five metres thick at the base, it's still an impressive structure, and boasts the distinction of being the one and only Norman fortification in Wales never to have fallen at one point or other to the insurgent armies of the Welsh princes.

On a January day in 1457 a 13-year-old girl, recently widowed, gave birth to a baby boy within the castle walls. She was Margaret Beaufort and her fatherless son was Henry Tudor. He returned to his birthplace 28 years later with a largely French invasion force, marched into England and defeated Richard III to claim the crown of England.

The ride leaves Pembroke heading west on quiet lanes skirting past the smokestacks of the

---

START & FINISH: Pembroke • DISTANCE: 31 miles/50km • TOTAL ASCENT: 589m
TERRAIN: Lanes plus a 3 mile section on a gravel path. Moderate

Pembroke Castle

Castlemartin firing range

Pembroke oil refinery. Further along is the Devil's Quoit, a Bronze Age cromlech comprising some truly whopping stones. Five thousand years ago it would have been a place of ritual significance and I wonder what the people who built it would make of the oil refinery that's sprung up just a few fields away. The route continues west through the sand dune landscape of Broomhill Burrows.

In the early 1100s Flemish settlers from present day Belgium and Holland came to Pembrokeshire, fleeing their low-lying lands after catastrophic storms. As a result, Pembrokeshire came to be known as 'Little England Beyond Wales' and developed its own English dialect. Among nearly 2,000 words and expressions are some real gems. 'Catamouse' means bat and 'frost candle' means icicle. Someone fit and athletic is a 'long dogs' while 'balshag' means scruff-bag. Even today, there's a clear linguistic-cultural divide separating 'the north' (Welsh) from 'down below' (Anglo-Flemish).

Heading inland you go through Castlemartin and into the Castlemartin military training area. Do check ahead for firing times, but most weekends are fine. The road ends atop the cliffs overlooking the precipitous limestone pillars of Elegug Stacks from where you follow the wide gravel path along the cliffs. Slowly decaying among the wildflowers are the burnt out remains of tanks and military vehicles, a reminder that this place has been used as an army training area since the Second World War. At the end of the track is the path down to St Govan's chapel. Wedged impossibly into the cliffs, it is one of the most remarkable buildings on the entire Welsh coastline, dedicated to the sixth-century hermit who lived here in a cave.

The sandy beach at nearby Broad Haven South is perfect for an afternoon dip and the return leg is a moderately hilly run along quiet lanes through Bosherston, Stackpole and Cheriton, the salty coastal vibe giving way to lush woodland before a long, relaxing descent back to Pembroke.

Download route info at thebikeshow.net/22CC

PUBS & PIT STOPS

OLD POINT HOUSE, Angle Point SA71 5AS (01646 641205) Popular pub right on Angle Bay.

ST GOVAN'S INN, Bosherston SA71 5DN (01646 661311) Country inn with rooms.

STACKPOLE WALLED GARDEN CAFÉ, Stackpole Estate SA71 5DJ (01646 661442) Café serving food grown in this historic kitchen garden.

STACKPOLE INN. Jason's Corner, Stackpole, SA71 5DF (01646 672324) Pretty pub, award-winning food, rooms.

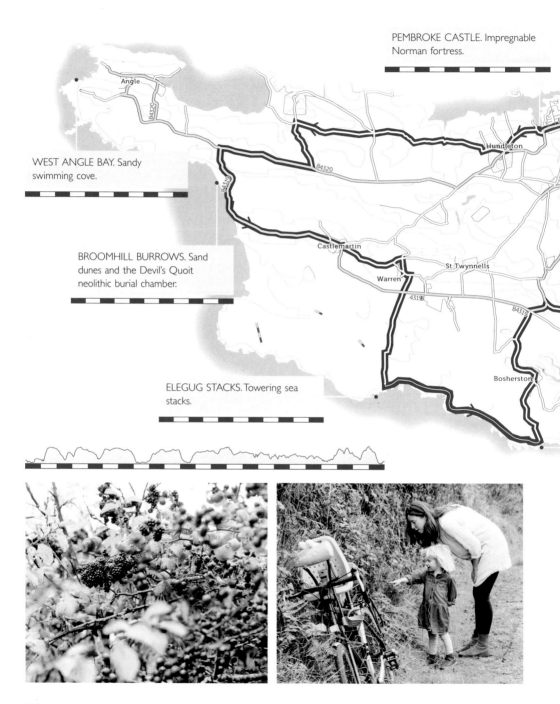

PEMBROKE CASTLE. Impregnable Norman fortress.

WEST ANGLE BAY. Sandy swimming cove.

BROOMHILL BURROWS. Sand dunes and the Devil's Quoit neolithic burial chamber.

ELEGUG STACKS. Towering sea stacks.

BROAD HAVEN SOUTH. Sandy beach; lily pond nature trail nearby.

ST GOVAN'S CHAPEL. Cliff-edge chapel and hermit cave.

BORDERS

No.23

CASTLES AND COBBLES

A ride out into the flatlands of the Cheshire plain, with plenty of interesting architecture along the way

———

For such a small city, Chester enjoys an embarrassment of riches. From Roman remains that include Britain's largest amphitheatre to the almost completely intact medieval city walls; from its hulking cathedral to its Norman castle; the River Dee to the network of canals; from its zoo, the largest in Britain; to its racecourse, the smallest and oldest. The Rows, Chester's unique double decker shopfronts, are medieval in design but they're not as old as they look – most are Victorian imitations in a medieval style – but they are still a fantastic way to shop. No wonder the architecture critic Ian Nairn confessed to being in love with the city.

This ride heads southeast from the city across pan-flat farmland to the sandstone ridge of the Peckforton Hills. Chester's river, the Dee, flows north to Liverpool Bay and the city thrived as a port for many centuries until eventually its harbour silted up. Canals came to the rescue and kickstarted the growth of industrial Chester. This aspect of the city is on show on the route out of town, along the Shropshire Union Canal towpath, past towering red brick Steam Mill, shot tower and water tower. It gets into countryside surprisingly quickly and a long, narrow lane leads through an avenue of oak trees to the three tiny cobblestone bridges known as Hockenhull Platts. A historic crossing of marshes of the River Gowy, it is hard to believe that for many

years this was the main road between London and Chester. Many notable travellers passed here, from Edward, the Black Prince, who paid for the repair of the bridges in 1353, to Celia Fiennes who encountered highwaymen here in 1698. A 19th century road-building plan would have seen the bridges demolished but for the intervention of the Marquess of Westminster, who owned the land.

The route works its way east to Tarpoley, a handsome, well-heeled village that was once on the main route between London and Chester (stop in for a drink or a bite at the Swan, a grand old coaching house). It's then over the canal towards Beeston Castle. If the castle, perched high on a sandstone crag, looks like a Crusader fortress dropped onto the Cheshire plain, it may be because it was built in the 1220s by Ranulf de Blondeville, Earl of Chester, fresh back from fighting in the Holy Land.

The castle stands at the northeastern tip of the Peckforton Hills and the next section of the route weaves its way past Peckforton Castle, a faux castle that's actually a Victorian country house, then along the range. Crossing the ridge includes an unexpected cobbled lane whose primitive pavé exceeds the worst of Flanders' famed cobbled climbs – in other words, it is unrideable. At the southwestern end of the ridge stands Maiden

---

START & FINISH: Chester • DISTANCE: 42 miles/67km • TOTAL ASCENT: 567m
TERRAIN: Lanes and two short cobbled sections. Moderate

Hockenhull Platts

Castle, one of seven Iron Age hill forts in Cheshire, though it's not really visible from the road.

Far away to the west rise the Welsh hills, and the border is the next destination as the ride meanders its way through a series of neat, red-bricked villages. The conjoined villages of Farndon and Holt stand either side of the River Dee, the crossing point from England to Wales, where the river has forced its way through sandstone cliffs. This deep, reddish pink stone was laid down a quarter of a billion years ago when much of the earth was a hot, barren desert after the Permian extinction had wiped out upwards of 90 per cent of plant and animal species. The bridge is an eight-arch stunner and may date as far back as the 1330s.

Resisting the desire to cross into Wales, the route instead heads north on lanes, avoiding all but a short section of the B5130, and enters the heart of the Duke of Westminster's domain. The richest member of the British aristocracy, the Duke's fortune exceeds even the Queen's. His Grosvenor Estate covers not just vast swathes of prime Cheshire farmland but much of the plush London districts of Mayfair and Belgravia, the latter taking it name from Belgrave, a nearby Cheshire village. Aldford is a red brick model village for workers on the Duke's estate and it's built in a distinctively eclectic Victorian style: Gothic revival with Jacobean flourishes.

From Aldford it's a direct return via Saighton, Waverton and back onto the canal into Chester. Any remaining time and energy could be spent on a circuit of the city walls. Just follow the canal until it meets the Dee, turn left and continue along the riverside path beneath the city walls, past the the racecourse and onto the promenade. Head back into the city centre at the far end of Grosvenor Park, on Dee Lane.

Download route info at thebikeshow.net/23CC

PUBS & PIT STOPS

THE SWAN, 50 High Street, Tarporley CW6 0AG (01829 733838) Historic coaching inn, good food.

SHADY OAK, Bates Mill Lane, Beeston CW6 9UE. (07765 588748) Canalside pub and no frills campsite.

THE PHEASANT INN. Higher Burwardsley CH3 9PF (01829 770434) Oak-beamed inn with stunning views. Rooms available.

THE GREYHOUND, High Street, Farndon CH3 6PU (01829 270244) Village pub, real ale, B&B.

GROSVENOR ARMS, Chester Road, Aldford CH3 6HJ (01244 620228). Big red brick country pub on the Duke of Westminster's estate. Good food.

BIKE SHOP: Sixty Nine Cycles. Unit 4, Deva House, Lightfoot Street, Chester CH2 3AD (01244 347488)

BIKE HIRE: Chester Cycle Hire, 64 Hoole Road, Chester CH2 3NL (01244 351305)

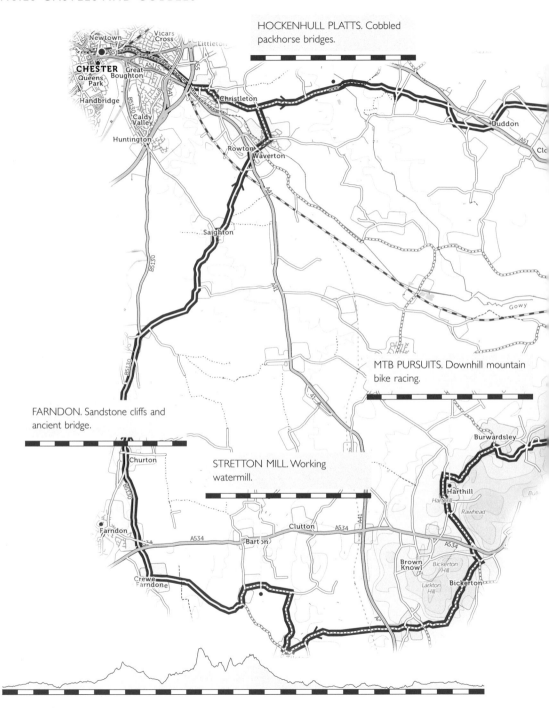

HOCKENHULL PLATTS. Cobbled packhorse bridges.

MTB PURSUITS. Downhill mountain bike racing.

FARNDON. Sandstone cliffs and ancient bridge.

STRETTON MILL. Working watermill.

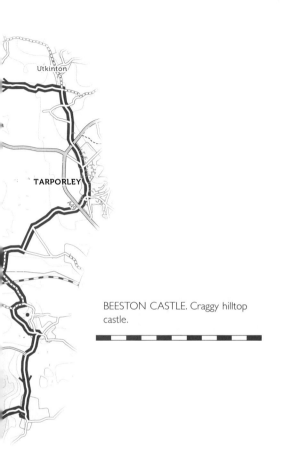

BEESTON CASTLE. Craggy hilltop castle.

No.24

ROCK OF AGES

A spectacular circumnavigation of the Long Mynd, the ancient colossus
at the heart of the Shropshire Hills

———

Shropshire has come a long way. Quite literally. Once upon a time (the technical term used by geologists is the Precambrian era) the county was 60 degrees south of the equator, further south even than the Falkland Islands. Shropshire perched on the edge of a very large continent where grinding tectonic plates and volcanic eruptions buckled and twisted the earth's crust. Then, as now, Shropshire was prone to the occasional rain shower, and geologists have found on the Long Mynd the presumed fossilised imprints of raindrops that fell 565 million years ago.

Shropshire was then flooded by a warm, shallow sea, and swimming about in that primordial soup were some of the earliest forms of life on earth. In the aeons that followed, Shropshire has risen out of the sea and been plunged back under, drifted northwards past the equator, seen both a tropical rainforest and a hot desert come and go. Finally, the whole area was covered by an ice sheet hundreds of metres thick. The eventual melting of this ice, and the water that ran off in streams and rivers, carved the shape of the hills that now rise from the gently rolling borderlands like giant humpbacked monsters.

This ride, a circuit of the Long Mynd, begins in Church Stretton, a quiet, genteel place with an alpine feel that's sometimes known as Little

Switzerland. The town gained national notoriety not long ago when a young resident with a drug habit and not long out of prison made a desperate phone call to the police begging to be arrested and sent back to jail. He said he was just so bored living out there "in the middle of nowhere". The police advised that he needed to commit a crime first so he obliged by going on a shoplifting spree at the local Waitrose.

Thrill-seeking cyclists will find this ride is just the ticket, taking in quiet lanes, panoramic views, challenging climbs and gripping descents. The ride begins by heading south through Little Stretton and Minton towards the crossing of the River Onny at Horderley. The first climb is up Ridgeway Hill to the village of Edgton. At the meeting of five roads and six footpaths and surrounded by hilltop forts, Edgton must once have been an important waypoint on long-distance routes. There is an early 19th century milestone that reads 'London 154 miles'. From this southerly vantage point the Long Mynd (long mountain) looks especially steep and impressive.

A few miles on, the village of Plowden is named for the local gentry who trace their lineage back to the 12th century and Roger de Plowden, a knight who served in the Crusades under Richard the Lionheart. Resisting the Protestant reforma-

---

START & FINISH: Church Stretton • DISTANCE: 27 miles/43km • TOTAL ASCENT: 920m
TERRAIN: Lanes and a short section of gravel track. Challenging

tion, the Plowdens retained their Catholic allegiance and built a little red brick Gothic chapel (St Walburga's) on the right-hand side of the lane as a place of worship for workers on the estate. After crossing the A489 the lane heads uphill, skirting the lower slopes of the Long Mynd, with fine views west towards Corndon Hill and the Stiperstones. From Wentnor the route follows the eastern branch of the River Onny upstream.

Ratlinghope is a settlement dating back to Saxon times. In the graveyard of the village church lies the body of Richard Munslow, the last known 'sin-eater' in England, who died in 1906. Sin-eaters were hired by bereaved families to eat food and drink that had been placed on or near the body of the deceased. They believed this act would transfer to the sin-eater any unconfessed or unforgiven sins that might be preventing their loved one from entering the kingdom of heaven. A small fee was paid to the sin-eater, who was often a pauper or a social outcast. With each ceremony the soul of the sin-eater was said to become ever more defiled. Ratlinghope is also home to a small annual music festival organised by a local farmer named Phil and known imaginatively enough as Farmer Phil's.

From Ratlinghope, the route follows Darnford Brook up onto the summit plateau of the Long Mynd. Here are two of the largest and best preserved of the dozens of Bronze Age barrows, tumuli and earthworks on the Mynd. It's a wild, windswept and disorienting landscape and it was here, 150 years ago, that the Reverend E. Donald Carr, a local priest, spent 22 freezing hours wandering lost in heavy snowdrifts. Carr's account of his ordeal, entitled *A Night in the Snow*, became a best-seller.

At the summit, a right turn off the tarmacked road onto an unsurfaced track gives another perspective on the Long Mynd (if you're averse to unsurfaced paths, carry straight on). It's soon back onto the road for the white-knuckle descent into Carding Mill valley and back to Church Stretton.

Download route info at thebikeshow.net/24RA

PUBS & PIT STOPS

BERRY'S, 17 High St, Church Stretton SY6 6BU (01694 724452) Small café serving great local food.

VAN DOESBURG'S, 3 High Street, Church Stretton SY6 6BU (01694 722867) Gourmet picnic provisions.

HOUSEMANS. 27 High Street, Church Stretton SY6 6BX (01694 724441) Popular modern European bistro.

GREEN DRAGON, Ludlow Road, Little Stretton SY6 6RE (01694 722925) Friendly village pub, excellent food.

SMALL BATCH CAMPSITE. Little Stretton SY6 6PW (01694 723358) Scenic family-run campsite, pubs nearby.

THE BRIDGES, Ratlinghope, SY5 0ST (01588 650260) Riverside pub run by The Three Tuns brewery. B&B.

BROW FARM CAMPSITE, Ratlinghope SY5 0SR (01588 650641) Campsite in 12 acres of meadows.

VICTORIA HOUSE. 48 High Street, Church Stretton SY6 6BX (01694 723823) Lovely B&B and café.

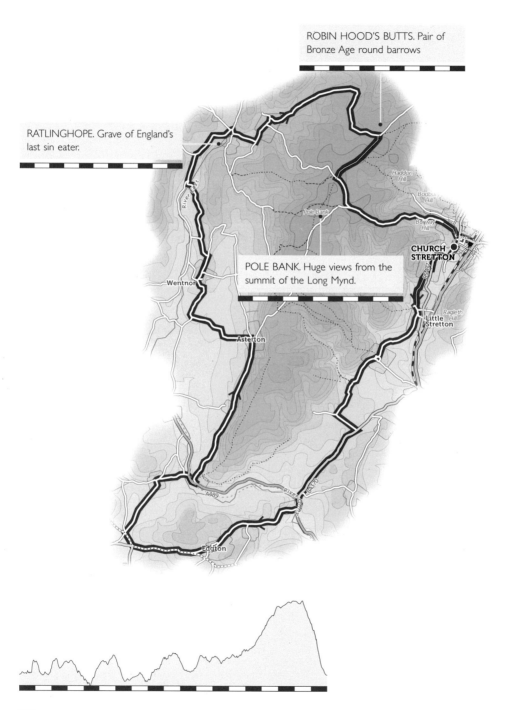

ROBIN HOOD'S BUTTS. Pair of Bronze Age round barrows

RATLINGHOPE. Grave of England's last sin eater.

POLE BANK. Huge views from the summit of the Long Mynd.

Haddon Hill

Bodbury Hill

Pole Bank

Bulway Hill

CHURCH STRETTON

Ragleth Hill

Little Stretton

Wentnor

Asterton

A489

Eqqton

No.25

BLUE REMEMBERED HILLS

From 'the country for easy livers, the quietest under the sun'
to the windblown heights of the Kerry Ridgeway

———

There are no more romantic characters in the long history of Wales and the Borders than the drovers. With its hilly terrain and heavy weather, Welsh farming has always been more about livestock than cereals. The main markets for Welsh livestock were English towns and cities and, before the railways, farmers entrusted their beasts to professional drovers, who made the long journeys with large groups of beasts. Most famously they drove herds of small but sturdy Welsh Black cattle but also sheep, pigs and sometimes even geese.

To fetch the highest prices, drovers had to get animals to market in the best possible condition, and they were talented wayfarers with a deep knowledge of the landscape, the routes, how to steer clear of robbers and rustlers, and the best stopping places to feed, rest and water their animals. Drovers were a vital link between towns and cities and remote rural homesteads. They carried the news, and their system of credit notes was an early form of rural banking.

Most drove roads simply followed well-trodden paths along the valley floor, which have since evolved into main roads, all evidence of their past use lost under the asphalt. However, plenty of upland drove roads remain. Drovers certainly used the cross-border ridgeway route from Kerry to Bishop's Castle, but the route is actually far older,

dating back to prehistoric times. Most of the route is a bridleway and though open to bikes, it can get exceptionally muddy. This ride takes in a portion that's on lanes with a short gravel section that is perfectly passable on touring bikes.

The ride is a 40km loop from Bishop's Castle but anyone travelling by train will need to start at Craven Arms and ride west to join the route. There are two ways to do this: either by following National Cycle Route 44 east along quiet though hilly lanes via Lydbury North to join the route at Brockton, or by taking the flatter but busier B4368 and joining the route at Clun. These extra legs to and from Craven Arms bring the total distance to around 65km.

Bishop's Castle is one of those precious small market towns with a strong sense of itself and it has resisted homogenisation by the bland and depressingly familiar retail chains. Overlooking the steeply pitched High Street is a handsome medieval town hall. A little further uphill is the site of the fortification that gives the town its name. All that remains today is a wall but several nearby buildings, including the Castle Hotel, were built with stone salvaged from the ruins. Around the corner is the Three Tuns Brewery. Founded in 1642 it's among Britain's oldest, and during the dark decades of industrially produced keg bitter,

---

START & FINISH: Bishops Castle • DISTANCE: 24 miles/39km • TOTAL ASCENT: 654m
TERRAIN: Lanes, two fairly short off-road sections, can be muddy after heavy rain. Easy

Bishops Castle

breweries like this kept alive the flickering flame of real ale, long before anyone coined the term 'micro-brewery'.

From Bishop's Castle the route heads south via Brockton and up to Bury Ditches, a massive Iron Age hill fort. It's defended by concentric rings of ditches and ramparts that would originally have reached up to seven metres high. The route skirts the summit on unsurfaced forestry tracks, and it's a short walk to the very top from where there are huge views in every direction. The route rejoins surfaced lanes at Guilden Down for the steep descent into Clun. This is a small, tranquil town, one of A. E. Housman's "quietest places under the sun". It is centred around a 500-year-old hump-backed packhorse bridge that joins Saxon Clun (south bank, around the church) with Norman Clun (north bank, around the castle). In the 19th century the town was able to support a staggering

16 artisan bootmakers' workshops and ten tailors until factory-made shoes from the Midlands put most of them out of business. John Osborne, the playwright whose *Look Back In Anger* was an earthquake moment in 20th century theatre, lived nearby and is buried in the churchyard.

From Clun the route heads west on the north bank of the River Clun, across Offa's Dyke to Newcastle, where it heads uphill on a long ascent into the wild uplands of the Clun Forest. This was once a vast expanse of heath and heather moor but most of it was lost to the plough in the 1940s as wartime Britain dug for victory. At the top, the route joins the Kerry Ridgeway, initially on an unsurfaced track then on lanes and back over Offa's Dyke, for the gentle descent along one of Britain's oldest drove ways for the last miles back to Bishop's Castle.

Download route info at thebikeshow.net/25BR

PUBS & PIT STOPS

THE THREE TUNS. 16 Market Square, Bishops Castle SY9 5BN (01588 638392) Historic brewery and keeper of the real ale flame.

THE PORCH HOUSE. 33 - 35 High Street, Bishops Castle SY9 5BE (01588 638854) Beautiful Elizabethan half-timbered house. B&B and self-catering apartments.

TEA ON THE WAY, Guilden Down Cottage, just past Bury Ditches (07795 275557) Home-made garden teas, fine views. Friday-Monday only.

THE MALTINGS, 12 High Street, Clun SY7 8JB. (01588 640539) Cheerful café, good vegetarian options.

THE SUN INN, Clun SY7 8JB (01588 640559) 15th century inn now owned by the local Three Tuns Brewery. B&B.

THE WHITE HORSE INN, Clun SY7 8JA (01588 640305) 18th century coaching inn and post house. Cyclist-friendly B&B.

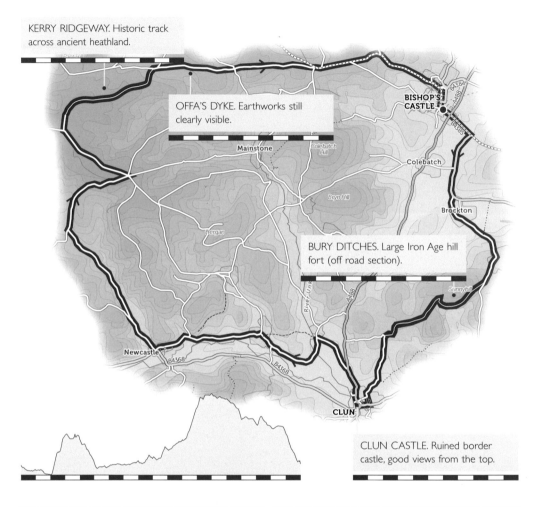

KERRY RIDGEWAY. Historic track across ancient heathland.

OFFA'S DYKE. Earthworks still clearly visible.

BURY DITCHES. Large Iron Age hill fort (off road section).

BISHOP'S CASTLE

CLUN

CLUN CASTLE. Ruined border castle, good views from the top.

Offa's Dyke

Clun Castle

No.26

MORTIMER COUNTRY

A ride from Ludlow, gastronomic capital of England, into the lands of the medieval Marcher lords

———

Picture yourself as the young Roger de Mortimer, Earl of March. It's the early 14th century and you're standing on the battlements of Ludlow Castle, the fortress citadel at the heart of your fiefdom. All the land you can see is yours, and much more besides. But what you cannot see is the future. King Edward II will make you his right-hand man in Ireland, where you'll triumph in battle. But soon after you'll lead an insurrection against the king and end up a prisoner in the Tower of London. You'll make a daring escape and flee to France with the king's wife, whom you'll take as your mistress. Together you'll return to England, depose the king and for three years you'll rule England and amass vast wealth and lands. But your young stepson Edward III will seek to avenge his father and you'll die, aged 43, on the gallows at Tyburn.

It's the kind of fast paced, high-stakes life story that would appeal to the writer and film-maker Jonathan Meades, who also loves this corner of Shropshire. "It doesn't have the regular provincial chip about not being London," he writes, "but then it's not provincial – it feels autonomous, devolved, independent. It's like a de facto state, it's an English Andorra. And Ludlow is its capital."

He's right. Ludlow is the lost capital of Wales and the Borders. Centuries after Roger Mortimer

came to a sticky end, the town was the seat of the heir to the English throne, the Prince of Wales. The royal court and the town's wealth from the wool trade have long set Ludlow apart from other border towns. It is now famed for its food culture and its wealth of fine buildings, medieval and Georgian. Besides the castle there is the church of St Laurence, nicknamed the 'Cathedral of the Marches', the flamboyantly half-timbered Feathers Hotel and the classical stone Buttercross.

This ride takes a tour of Mortimer's Shropshire, and Meades' too, the English Andorra. It begins by heading south along the River Teme before crossing the A49 by bridge and heading up Tinker's Hill, crossing the Teme once more at Ashford Carbonell. A climb through Batchcott leads to Richard's Castle, one of the earliest Norman castles built to defend the English border with Wales. It's now an overgrown ruin, but the church beside it is intact and well worth a poke around inside. On a clear day you can see the Malvern Hills to the south-east and the Black Mountains to the south-west. The forest of tall, slim radio towers is the Woofferton transmission station, the last shortwave transmitters left in Britain, broadcasting the BBC World Service. During the Cold War, Woofferton beamed the *Voice of America* to listeners

---

START & FINISH: Ludlow • DISTANCE: 37 miles/59km • TOTAL ASCENT: 888m
TERRAIN: Lanes. Moderate

Hopton Castle

in the Eastern bloc with a signal beefy enough to overcome the Soviet radio jammers.

It's a short descent onto Leinthall Moor, a pan-flat river basin that was once a glacial lake. The farmland here floods regularly and I've seen some of the lanes submerged under six inches of water. Near Burrington it's back over the meandering River Teme, this time considerably upstream of Ludlow, and a short ride on to Leintwardine, a large, good-looking village with more than 2,000 years of history. The conquering Romans established a military staging post here, on the road between the city of Viroconium (Wroxeter) and the legionary fortress at Isca (Caerleon). A Romano-British town grew up here, named Bravonium.

From Leintwardine it's a ride across the floodplain of the River Clun to Bedstone and Hopton Castle. The narrow lane that skirts around Clunbury Hill offers Tolkeinesque views up the Clun valley. It's then back east through Aston on Clun and Broome. The climb up to View Edge is a brute but, as the name hints, the panorama from the top is worth the effort. After a long descent to the River Onny at Onibury it's an easy ride along the river all the way back to Ludlow. The final section, on largely traffic-free lanes through Oakly Park, is a real treat that culminates in a dramatic reveal of Ludlow Castle. But who's the solitary figure standing on the battlements?

Download route info at thebikeshow.net/26MC

PUBS & PIT STOPS

HARP LANE DELI, 4 Church Street, Ludlow SY8 1AP (01584 877353) Gourmet picnic provisions.

VAUGHAN'S, 14 King Street, Ludlow (01584 875453) Much-loved sandwich bar specialising in local meats.

THE GREEN CAFÉ, Dinham Bridge, Ludlow (01584 879872) Riverside café, seasonal food.

THE SUN INN, Rosemary Lane, Leintwardine SY7 0LP (01547 540705) One of England's last parlour pubs.

THE LION, Leintwardine SY7 0JZ (01547 540203) Riverside dining pub, B&B.

THE APPLE TREE, Onibury SY7 9AW (01584 856633) Relaxed pub serving simple, home-cooked local food.

THE FEATHERS, The Bull Ring, Ludlow SY8 1AA (01584 875261) Stay in one of the greatest buildings in England.

THE CHURCH INN, King Street, Ludlow SY8 1AW (01584 872174) Perfect local for a post-ride pint.

BIKE SHOP: Epic Cycles, Weeping Cross Lane, Ludlow SY8 1PA (01584 879245)

BIKE HIRE: Wheely Wonderful Cycling. Petchfield Farm, Elton SY8 2HJ. (01568 770755) Can arrange delivery.

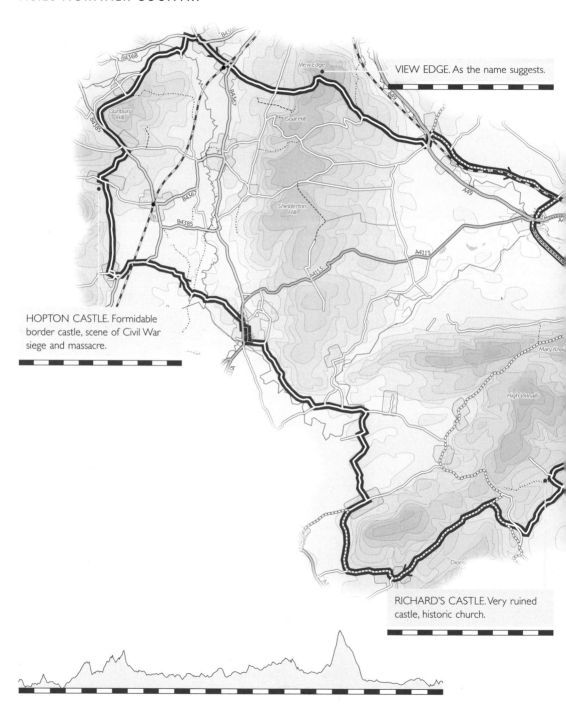

VIEW EDGE. As the name suggests.

HOPTON CASTLE. Formidable border castle, scene of Civil War siege and massacre.

RICHARD'S CASTLE. Very ruined castle, historic church.

LUDLOW CASTLE. Imposing
Mortimer family stronghold.

WOOD FROM THE TREES

From the quintessential English market town of Leominster to the wild Welsh border,
on the trail of the black and white villages

When it comes to woodland, Britain is now the bald man of Europe. Once upon a time, vast primeval forests covered almost the whole of the British Isles. Today trees account for just 12 per cent of the land area, compared to about one-third in France and Germany and a whopping 73 per cent in Finland. Yet Britain is blessed with the lion's share of northern Europe's ancient, veteran and champion trees, or as 19th century English clergyman Francis Kilvert described them, "those grey, gnarled, low browed, knock kneed, bent, huge, strange, long armed, deformed, hunch-backed, misshapen oak men that stand awaiting and watching century after century".

As Kilvert would have known, nowhere is Britain's wealth of ancient trees more evident than in the Welsh Borders. And not just standing tall in the fields and hedgerows, but used in the construction of the half-timbered buildings that are the most distinctive aspect of the local architecture. The black and white villages of the Herefordshire/ Shropshire border have long been marketed as a tourist attraction, a vision of 'Merrie England'. I've always found this a bit strange since the black and white villages were only painted black and white in the mid-19th century. Before that, the timbers would have been left their natural colour or very lightly lime-washed. The walls between would have

been the colour of the local clay, ranging from soft pinks to mild ambers. There is still plenty of black and white to be found, but many owners of these historic buildings are now reverting to the old ways by revealing the natural hues and grain of the timber, and showcasing all the better the fine work of the craftsmen who built them.

This ride begins in Leominster, a market town whose many fine half-timbered buildings owe their existence to the medieval wool trade that saw the town prosper, literally off the backs of local Ryeland sheep. Their soft, short wool, known as 'Lemster ore', was highly prized and Queen Elizabeth I insisted on it for her woollen stockings. With the coming of the industrial revolution Leominster switched from wool to cotton, and more recently it has evolved into the antiques shop capital of the Borders.

This ride is a loop west to Kington, not far from the border with Wales. To begin, the route follows the course of the River Lugg through Eyton and Kingsland on quiet lanes and the B road to Eardisland, a picture-perfect village astride the River Arrow complete with a moated castle ruin, a couple of pubs, a tea room and a 17th century dovecote that now plays host to a community shop.

It's then a back lanes route over the A44 to Pembridge, perhaps the quintessential black and

---

START & FINISH: Leominster • DISTANCE: 46 miles/73km • TOTAL ASCENT: 631m
TERRAIN: Lanes. Moderate

Eardisland

white village. Its current population of around 1,000 is half its peak in the Middle Ages, when the town was one of the trading posts where English wool merchants and Welsh sheep farmers would meet to do business in safety. The stocky church, with its separate bell tower, hints at the importance of Pembridge in its heyday.

From Pembridge wiggly lanes roughly shadow the River Arrow west, picking up the B4355 for the run-in to Kington. Despite being on the western (Welsh) side of Offa's Dyke, Kington has been firmly English since before the Norman conquest. The place has a medieval feel and was a staging point for drovers heading east over Hergest Ridge. Heading west out of Kington, the route traces the ridge's lower contours. It's a wild, windswept hill said to be haunted by a ghost dog. In the early 1970s the spectral hound was joined by prog rock multi-instrumentalist Mike Oldfield, who moved here in search of peace and isolation after he found stardom with Tubular Bells. His follow-up album was a paean to Hergest Ridge, where he used to fly his model gliders.

Crossing the River Arrow, it's a bit of a slog up to the top of Brilley Mountain from where a confusing web of narrow farm lanes leads to Eardisley. This was once a stop on the Hay Railway, a very early horse-drawn goods line that connected Brecon with Kington, and some of the railway buildings remain. Heading back to Leominster, the route wends its way along lanes through three final black and white villages: Almeley, Weobley (pronounced Web-ley) and Dilwyn.

Download route info at thebikeshow.net/27WT

PUBS & PIT STOPS

RITA'S TEAROOM, Eardisland HR6 9BD (01544 388064) Good breakfasts, light lunches and teas.

NEW INN, Market Square, Pembridge HR6 9DZ (01544 388427) Ancient, half-timbered inn in the heart of the village.

YE OLDE STEPPES, High Street, Pembridge HR6 9DS (01544 388506) Award-winning shop & tea rooms.

THE CIDER BARN, Bearwood Lane, Pembridge HR6 9ED (01544 388161) Top-notch food at organic cider mill.

THE STAGG INN, Titley HR5 3RL (01544 230221) First British pub to win a Michelin star. Rooms available.

BORDER BEAN, 22-24 High St. Kington HR5 3AX (01544 231625) Cheery independent coffee shop.

CHURCH HOUSE, Church Rd, Kington HR5 3AG (01544 230534) Tranquil, elegant B&B.

RHODDS BARN, Lyonshall HR5 3LW (01544 340120) Plush barn in two acres of stunning gardens. Sleeps 4.

THE TRAM INN. Church Road, Eardisley HR3 6PG (01544 327251) Half-timbered, quarry-tiled freehouse serving good, simple food.

JULES, Portland Street, Weobley HR4 8SB (01544 318206) Stylish eaterie serving good local food, popular with cyclists

OLD FORGE TEA ROOM, Dilwyn HR4 8HL (01544 319306) Teas in a beautiful village.

BIKE SHOP: Phill Prothero Cycles, 91-93 Etnam Street, Leominster HR6 8AF (01568 611222)

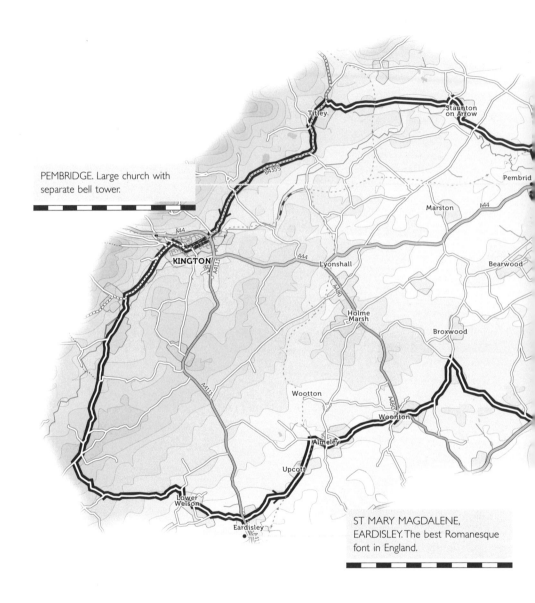

PEMBRIDGE. Large church with separate bell tower.

ST MARY MAGDALENE, EARDISLEY. The best Romanesque font in England.

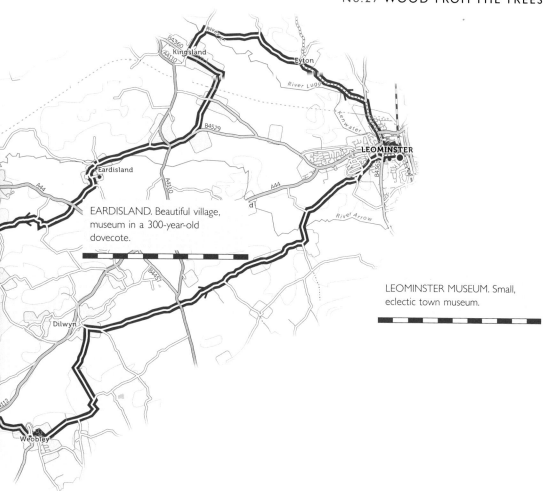

EARDISLAND. Beautiful village, museum in a 300-year-old dovecote.

LEOMINSTER MUSEUM. Small, eclectic town museum.

No.28

RED PLANET

A tour of southern Herefordshire, from the meandering River Wye
to the ridgeway on the border with Wales

If counties had colours (and they have flags, mottos and coats of arms, so it doesn't seem too far-fetched) then the official colour of Herefordshire would be a rich, dusky pink. It's the colour you see in the wild rocky outcrops and dark river gorges, in ploughed fields and in the tracks and pathways that criss-cross the rolling landscape.

Herefordshire lies at the centre of a large belt of Old Red Sandstone some 400 million years old. It is made of compressed mud and silt, and the reddish hue derives from tiny particles of oxidised iron. Many of Herefordshire's most celebrated buildings are made of the stuff and this ride takes in several of them, starting right in front of one of the best, the Market House in Ross-on-Wye. In medieval times, most market towns in Wales and the Borders were centred upon such a building, with an open-walled ground floor and rooms above. Some are in stone, others are in timber. Many have been demolished by misguided town planners and the few that remain should be cherished.

Perched on a bluff above a wide bend in the River Wye, Ross is one of those handsome market towns with several traditional butchers, some great independent shops selling books and antiques, and a fantastic deli. Although it lacks a railway station, the town makes a perfect base for exploring the area, either on two wheels or by hiring a canoe and paddling downstream.

The route starts by tracing a wide meander of the Wye on some exceptionally scenic lost lanes all the way to the bridge at Hoarwithy. There's an adventurous alternative route to Hoarwithy which involves two crossings of the Wye on the footbridges at Foy and Sellack (passing en route the sandstone-spired church at Sellack). This alternative includes some short stretches on footpaths where bikes should be walked and which are best undertaken in summer when the fields are dry.

From Hoarwithy the road heads upwards, gently at first, and then, after crossing the A466, steeply up Orcop Hill. From here you can see for miles and miles across the entire county. It's downhill to Kilpeck and what Simon Jenkins describes as "England's most perfect Norman church". Built from Old Red Sandstone, it is a showcase for the talents of the Hereford School of stonemasons who developed a flamboyant Romanesque style all of their own. The columned archway around the south door is mesmerising while the outside walls host a motley collection of grotesques, including an upside down pig, a dog and rabbit that look straight out of a *Wallace and Gromit* cartoon, a pair of doves, musicians, wrestlers, acrobats and an excellent, horribly lewd

---

START & FINISH: Ross-on-Wye • DISTANCE: 43 miles/68km • TOTAL ASCENT: 1013m
TERRAIN: Lanes. Challenging

Kilpeck church

sheela-na-gig. The stonework looks as fresh as if it had been carved yesterday, and it's a miracle the carvings survived the Puritan vandals of the 17th century. Less well-preserved is the Norman castle next door, now no more than a few crumbling walls, but an atmospheric spot affording good views all around.

From Kilpeck, the route heads back up to Bagwyllydiart and Garway Hill. This is the hilliest part of the ride but the rewards are yet more breathtaking views: north over the Hereford plain and the Golden Valley, and west to the steep northern escarpment of the Black Mountains. In the time of the Crusades, Garway was a regional centre for the Knights Templar and it's worth losing a little altitude for a short detour to see

Garway church with its fortified tower and more Hereford School carvings, or to visit the gardens at Kentchurch Court. Near Garway church is a massive stone dovecote. Built in 1326 it's the oldest recorded freestanding dovecote in Britain and considered by connoisseurs of the *columbarium* to be among the best.

The road to Welsh Newton passes Pembridge Castle, an imposing border castle in yet more Old Red Sandstone. The final run back to Ross-on-Wye goes through fruit orchards around Glewstone and there's a chance to taste the artisan cider and perry produced at Broome Farm if you stop at the Yew Tree Inn at Peterstow.

Download route info at thebikeshow.net/28RP

PUBS & PIT STOPS

TRUFFLES DELI, 46 High Street, Ross-on-Wye HR9 5GH (01989 762336) Superior picnic provisions.

NEW HARP INN, Hoarwithy HR2 6QH (01432 840900) Relaxed village pub with riverside camping.

KILPECK INN, Kilpeck HR2 9DN (01981 570464) Contemporary-styled pub. Real ales, food, B&B.

GARWAY MOON INN, Garway Common, Garway HR2 8RQ (01600 750270) Village pub and B&B.

THE BELL, Skenfrith NP7 8UH (01600 750235) Just off route, country hotel in an idyllic border village.

THE LOUGH POOL INN, Grove Common, Sellack HR9 6LX (01989 730888) Just off route, a good dining pub.

BROOME FARMHOUSE, Peterstow HR9 6QG (01989 562824) Good value B&B on a cider farm.

BIKE SHOP: Revolutions, 48 Broad Street, Ross-on-Wye HR9 7DY (01989 562639)

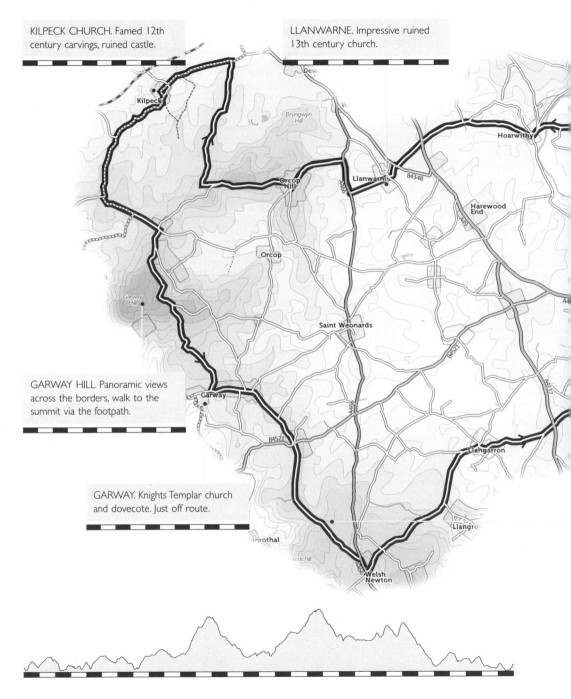

KILPECK CHURCH. Famed 12th century carvings, ruined castle.

LLANWARNE. Impressive ruined 13th century church.

GARWAY HILL. Panoramic views across the borders, walk to the summit via the footpath.

GARWAY. Knights Templar church and dovecote. Just off route.

Adventurous summertime alternative
route via Foy and Sellack. Walk
where necessary.

Garway Church

PEMBRIDGE CASTLE. Sandstone
castle, privately owned.

Garway Hill

IN RUINS

All the drama of the lower Wye valley and the bewitching remains
of 1,000 years of history

———

Why are ruins so captivating? For most of human history people saw ruins as nothing more than junk and mess. They were broken down and their stones used in other buildings, or repurposed as pigsties and cow byres. It was not until the 17th century that the first antiquarians took an interest in what ruins might tell us about the past. But a ruin also makes us think about the future. They remind us that nothing is forever, that decay is irresistible. It's a melancholic feeling to be standing on the tumbledown remains of a once-magnificent castle, abbey or stately home, imagining what once went on there. Likewise, to clamber into an old farmhouse, roof long since gone, and find a tree growing where the kitchen table once stood.

How did it come to this? What if the people who once lived there could see it now? No wonder the Romantic movement of the 18th century saw the ruin rise from eyesore to tourist destination and status symbol (it was quite common for the landed gentry to enhance their landscape gardens with fake ruins and grottoes). With war and revolution rendering the Greek and Roman ruins of the Grand Tour off-limits to the leisured elites, they started going instead to the lower Wye valley, with its swirling waters, rocky outcrops, steep-sided gorges and picturesque, ivy-clad ruins.

This ride follows a trail of ruins, starting at Chepstow, where the Norman cliff-top castle, begun barely a year after the Battle of Hastings, guards a strategic crossing point of the River Wye. Cyclists in Chepstow have long been campaigning for the old railway line up the Wye to be converted into a cycling and walking path, and this would make the journey up to Tintern Abbey a joy. But until that becomes a reality, the only option is on the A466 past the racecourse to St Arvans. It's a fast main road so not a particularly pleasant ride but fortunately there is a shared-use cycling and walking path beside it.

From St Arvans, the route follows the Devaulden Road (National Cycle Route 31) into Chepstow Park Wood, 3,300 acres of mixed woodland and once the hunting ground of Roger Bigod, an early medieval lord of Chepstow Castle. After a right turn towards the Cot, there's a long, winding descent down the steep-sided Angiddy valley, passing some of the ruins of ironworks that made this valley Wales's largest industrial complex in the 1600s. Edward Davies, the Chepstow poet, writing in 1804 spoke of where "black forges smoke, and noisy hammers beat… melting furnaces like Etna roar, and force the latent iron from the ore". It takes some imagination to picture it now.

———

START & FINISH: Chepstow • DISTANCE: 29 miles/47km • TOTAL ASCENT: 898m
TERRAIN: Lanes. Moderate

Trellech

St Mary's, Tintern

Runston chapel

Tintern Abbey, only the second Cistercian abbey established in the British Isles, dominated the local economy for 400 years, surviving violent power struggles between the monarch and the Marcher lords, the Welsh uprising of Owain Glyndŵr and even the Black Death. But Henry VIII's dissolution of the monasteries brought a swift end to monastic life in the valley. Iron masters soon took the place of monks, and Tintern's wireworks were up and running by the 1560s, making the lower Wye one of the incubators of Britain's industrial revolution.

The climb up from Tintern to Trellech featured in the national road race championship of 2014. More than a century earlier it was the scene of a spectacular bike crash involving George Bernard Shaw and Bertrand Russell. The pair were staying with socialists and writers Beatrice and Sidney Webb at the Argoed, a country house overlooking the Wye at Penallt, and it appears from the reports that Russell, aged 23 at the time, absentmindedly stopped to look at a signpost and was rear-ended by Shaw, who flew into the air and came to a halt five yards further down the hill. Shaw was able to ride home and in reports at the time the bearded man of letters "attributes his escape from serious consequences to the splendid quality of bone and muscle produced by vegetarian diet and Jaeger clothing".

Now a quiet village with a church, a pub and a village green, it's almost impossible to imagine that Trellech was once the largest settlement in medieval Wales, but that is exactly what the 'Lost City of Trellech' archeologists believe they are slowly uncovering. Continuing on through the villages and hamlets that dot the ridge between the Wye and the Usk rivers, the ride reaches Earlswood. From here there is a fabulous view of the River Severn, including the 'new' bridge opened in 1996 and beyond it the industrial sprawl of Avonmouth. One day all that will be ruins too, just like the village of Runston, the last ruin on this ride. All that remains of the medieval village is the chapel, roofless but with its Norman chancel arch perfectly intact. Tintern it's not, but it's nevertheless a moving place to stop and contemplate the nature of existence before the final downhill run to Chepstow.

Download route info at thebikeshow.net/29IR

PUBS & PIT STOPS

FILLING STATION CAFÉ, Main Road, Tintern NP16 6SF (07770 544592) Tiny café popular with local cyclists.

KINGSTONE BREWERY. Meadow Farm, Tintern NP16 7NX (01291 680111) Microbrewery, tap room and woodland glamping, just past Trelleck Road turn.

THE OLD STATION, Tintern NP16 7NX (01291 689566) Café in an old railway station. Riverside walks, just past Trelleck Road turn.

THE INN AT PENALLT, Penallt NP25 4SE (01600 772765). A few miles north of the route, country inn and B&B.

THE LION INN, Trelleck NP25 4PA (01600 860322) Village pub and B&B in an Elizabethan pig cot.

CARPENTERS ARMS, Mynydd Bach, Shirenewton NP16 6BU (01291 641231) Rambling pub in former village smithy.

BIKE SHOP: 559 Bikes, 4 Manor Way, Chepstow NP16 5HZ. (01291 626126)

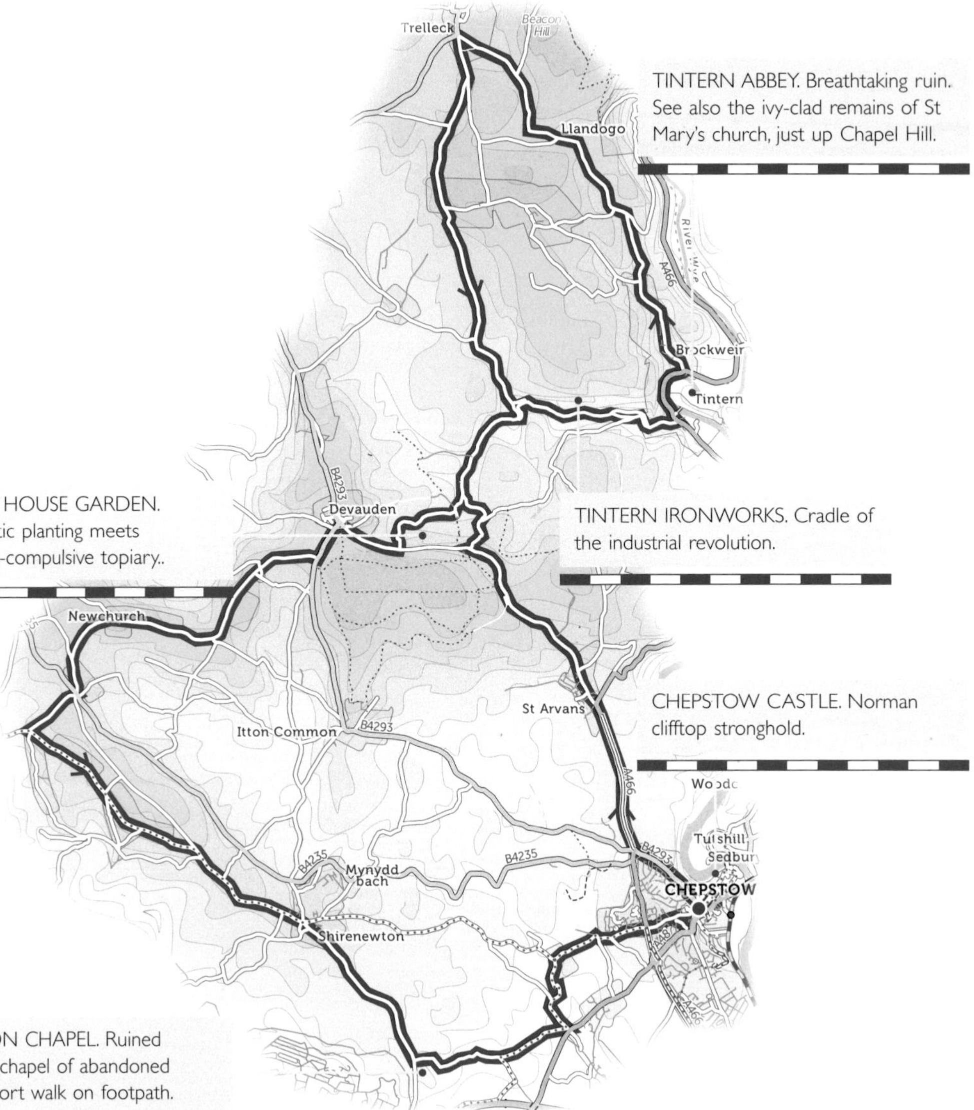
Trelleck
Beacon Hill
Llandogo
River Wye
A466
Tintern
B4293
Devauden
Newchurch
St Arvans
Itton Common
B4293
A466
B4293
B4235
Mynydd bach
B4235
Shirenewton
CHEPSTOW

TINTERN ABBEY. Breathtaking ruin. See also the ivy-clad remains of St Mary's church, just up Chapel Hill.

VEDDW HOUSE GARDEN. Naturalistic planting meets obsessive-compulsive topiary..

TINTERN IRONWORKS. Cradle of the industrial revolution.

CHEPSTOW CASTLE. Norman clifftop stronghold.

RUNSTON CHAPEL. Ruined Norman chapel of abandoned village, short walk on footpath.

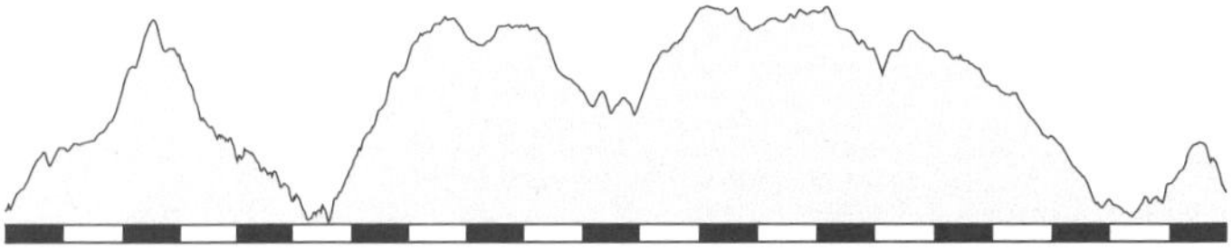

Glamping at Kingstone Brewery

DAFFODIL DREAMING

From the banks of the River Severn to the 'daffodil triangle', through the orchards, fields and meadows of western Gloucestershire

---

Among Welsh national symbols, the daffodil is a latecomer. The fashion for wearing the bright yellow springtime bloom to mark St David's Day on 1st March began with the Victorians. It was prettier and easier to wear than the leek, the traditional Welsh floral emblem, whose association with the Welsh goes back at least to Tudor times. The legend of the leek is that St David advised Welsh warriors to carry the green and white vegetable into battle to distinguish themselves from their Saxon foes.

But why the daffodil? Well, the Welsh for daffodil is *cenhinen bedr* - literally "(Saint) Peter's leek", so there may have been a linguistic misunderstanding along the way. Then again, daffodils bloom in March and early April, just in time for St David's Day. Daffodils grow wild throughout Wales, but mostly they're domesticated varieties that have escaped into the road verges. The dainty, diminutive wild daffodil *Narcissus pseudonarcissus* is much rarer, and the best place in Britain to see them is a few miles across the border in the north-west corner of Gloucestershire. The Great Western Railway once brought trainloads of tourists on Daffodil Specials to see fields and meadows carpeted in yellow. Since then, agricultural herbicides have eradicated the flowers from open land and they are now confined to a few woodland strongholds, roadside verges and a handful of unsprayed fields and meadows. But there are still plenty to see, and each spring the villages of Dymock, Kempley and Oxenhall host weekend festivals with guided daffodil walks and 'daffodil teas' in the village halls.

The ride starts in Gloucester, an ancient city on the banks of the River Severn. For centuries the first downstream crossing point of the Severn, the opening of a 16-mile-long ship canal in 1827 saw Gloucester docks teeming with tall ships, schooners, barges and barques. Little cargo is loaded here now – it's mostly leisure craft in the marina, while the wharfs and warehouses have since been made-over into apartments, offices, restaurants and bars.

The bike path across Alney Island nature reserve is a pleasure to ride, passing huge drifts of enormous bulrushes and dazzling flag irises, though after heavy rain it can be soft under wheel in places. The path continues up the Severn to Maisemore Bridge, a popular viewing point for the Severn Bore, a spectacular tidal surge that attracts surfers, windsurfers and canoeists to try their luck riding the big wave.

Maisemore is home to one of the country's biggest manufacturers of beekeeping paraphernalia and any passing bee enthusiast will also stop

---

START & FINISH: Gloucester • DISTANCE: 38 miles/61km • TOTAL ASCENT: 540m
TERRAIN: Lanes. Moderate

Gloucester docks

Bee shelter, Hartpury

in at Hartpury Court to see the remarkable and exquisitely carved stone bee shelter that's tucked away in the churchyard. For the fruit growers of the Vale of Leadon, bees are essential unpaid labour, pollinating the orchards that line the lanes around Upleadon, Botloe's Green and Oxenhall. After crossing the M50 motorway it's a short loop around the 'golden triangle' via Kempley Green and Dymock.

Besides the daffodils, the area is known as the place where a group of Edwardian poets made their homes in the years just before the First World War. Among the Dymock Poets were Robert Frost, Rupert Brooke and Edward Thomas. They all drew inspiration from the surrounding countryside and six miles due south of Dymock is May Hill, the highest point in Gloucestershire west of the Severn, visible from far and wide. Thomas wrote 'Words', one of his most celebrated poems, after a bike ride there. Though best known for his poetry, Thomas was also a travel writer. His book *In Pursuit of Spring* documents a solo bike ride he made from London to the West Country over Easter in 1913 and is one of the better examples of a much maligned genre, the cycling travelogue.

From Dymock the route heads back over the M50 and along more quiet lanes back to Maisemore, via Upleadon and Ashleworth. It's then just a matter of retracing your journey from earlier in the day down the Severn to Gloucester.

Download route info at thebikeshow.net/30DD

PUBS & PIT STOPS

BEAUCHAMP ARMS, Dymock GL18 2AQ (01531 890266) Great community-owned village pub.

THE BUTTERY TEA ROOM, 1 Culver St, Newent GL18 1DB (01531 820896) Small café does the best fry up in town.

THE BOAT INN, Ashleworth Quay GL19 4HZ (01452 700272) Fantastic little pub by the River Severn.

THREE CHOIRS VINEYARD, Castletump GL18 1LS (01531 890223) Vineyard and winery. Smart restaurant with valley views, B&B available.

PELERINE, Ford House Road, Newent GL18 1LQ (01531 822761) Small campsite, camp fires permitted.

BIKE SHOP: Eastgate Cycles, 76 - 78 Eastgate Street, Gloucester GL1 1QN (01452 300366)

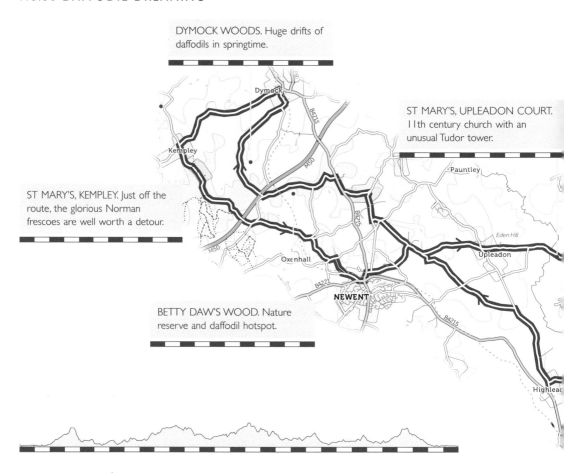

DYMOCK WOODS. Huge drifts of daffodils in springtime.

ST MARY'S, UPLEADON COURT. 11th century church with an unusual Tudor tower.

ST MARY'S, KEMPLEY. Just off the route, the glorious Norman frescoes are well worth a detour.

BETTY DAW'S WOOD. Nature reserve and daffodil hotspot.

St Mary's, Kempley

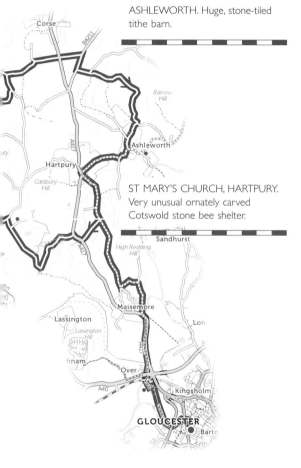

ASHLEWORTH. Huge, stone-tiled tithe barn.

ST MARY'S CHURCH, HARTPURY. Very unusual ornately carved Cotswold stone bee shelter.

OVER BRIDGE. Thomas Telford's 1828 stone span across the Severn.

Upleadon court

ORGANISED
RIDES

No. 31

WILD WALES CHALLENGE

The original, and still the best, mass-participation bike ride around
the mountainous landscape of North Wales

———

Describing itself as 'possibly the best kept cycling secret in the UK', the Wild Wales Challenge has been going for more than 30 years. It's not a race, it's not a sportive, it's just a great day out on the bike exploring some of North Wales's best cycling country – along with 650 of your newest best friends. The event is organised by Merseyside CTC and is in a long tradition of Liverpool-area cycling clubs making their way across to North Wales in search of fresh air and good riding.

The Liverpool Velocipede Club was Britain's first cycling club and was founded in 1869. Liverpool's Anfield Bicycle Club was founded a decade later and soon gained a reputation as the country's leading long-distance cycling club. Its first star rider was the record-breaking racer George Pilkington Mills, who rode from Lands End to John O'Groats in five days – on a penny farthing. He was the winner of the first Bordeaux-Paris race, held in 1891, and was part of the pioneering generation of road racers who inspired the Tour de France.

As befits its roots in cycling club culture, the Wild Wales Challenge has a very 'audax' feel about it, with little razzamatazz and no corporate sponsors but plenty of tea, cake and camaraderie. The route varies each year but is usually a little shy of 100 miles, which in the hilly country around the start and finish point in Bala is a big challenge for all but the fittest racing snakes. It is

significantly tougher than any of the rides in this book, not just because it's longer but because the total climbing is around 3,000m.

The £18 entry fee (in 2015) is low compared with most similar events, and covers changing facilities and showers at the start and finish, refreshments en route, a map and directions, a timer chip, marshals out on the route and access to a support vehicle manned by mechanics if things go wrong. All finishers receive a commemorative plaque made of Welsh slate.

Organiser Denis Holder says, "Any sort of bike may be ridden, as long as it's roadworthy". These days it's overwhelmingly a Lycra and road bike affair, which is understandable given the distance and terrain, but a fit touring cyclist looking to try a big one-day challenge will be quite welcome. Ultra-low touring gears will come in handy on the big climbs and a rider on a traditional touring bike with panniers or a saddlebag will be cheered around the course.

A well-run event with a great pedigree, it should be no surprise that the ride always sells out in advance. "We don't advertise it in the mags," says Denis. "We don't need to." Now you're in on the secret too.

Start/finish: Bala
Around 90 miles / 145 km
£18
www.wildwaleschallenge.com

CARDIFF TO THE BEACH NIGHT RIDE

A friendly, free, turn up-and-ride midsummer's adventure

One of the best cycling trends in the last decade is the rise of the night ride. Battery-powered bike lights have improved beyond recognition and people are realising that the roads are so much quieter at night. There's also an adventurous side to it, the thrill of doing something daring and different. Inspired by the Dunwich Dynamo, which has been running for more than twenty years, rides like Bristol's Exmouth Exodus, London's Midsummer Madness and the Friday Night Ride to the Coast series are now established events in their own right. And since 2013 Cardiff, too, has had its own summer night ride on the Saturday nearest the summer solstice. It starts at sunset from the centre of Cardiff and heads west for 67 miles to the Mumbles on Swansea Bay. The ride is a free, unsupported, turn-up-and-go event, which has got bigger each year. It attracts all kinds of riders, from people on sit-up-and-beg town bikes with wicker baskets to Lycra'd-up racing snakes on carbon fibre confections and everyone in between.

"It's a fairly flat route and will take however long you want it to", says organiser Ed Robson. "It depends on how fast you pedal and whether you stop off at any pubs on the way."

The allure of the night ride is hard to explain to the uninitiated. For much of the time it's dark, so you don't really see much beyond your immediate surroundings, but the pared-down, monochrome world has its own sensory delights, which start with the night sky. There's something dreamlike about riding under a pitch black, starlit sky, or when a full moon bathes the country-side in its soft, silvery light. The sodium glow of a distant town or city is always spectacular, especially if viewed from above. But it's not just what you see, but what you hear and feel when riding at night: the hunting cries and friendly hoots of owls, the eerie call of foxes, the fluttering wings of bats and the rustle of a hedgerow as a badger dives for cover. The air temperature varies much more at night than it does in the day – at least it feels that way – as you ride from the misty chill of a river valley into the inexplicable patches of warm air, rising thermals, maybe, that are gone almost as soon as they appear.

Every night ride is a journey into the unknown, and part of the challenge is just staying awake. There are inevitably dark moments of the soul, but the camaraderie of other riders is a big help and the coming of the dawn, at around 4am during the summer months, is always a salvation. The first riders arrive at the Mumbles in time to see the sun rise over Swansea Bay. After a refreshing dip in the sea and a restorative fried breakfast, it's a short train ride back to Cardiff.

Start: Y Mochyn Du pub, Cardiff. CF11 9HW
Finish: The Mumbles, Swansea
Free
67 miles / 108 km
www.facebook.com/events/666899600035713

VELOTHON WALES

Wales's newest, biggest and glitziest cyclosportive, from Cardiff to the Brecon Beacons and back

Every year sees a new record set for the number of cyclists who take part in cyclosportives on British roads. Sportives, as they're more often known, are 'timed challenge' cycling events which aren't races but, for many of the participants, they have a semi-competitive, race-like feel about them. It's all very much linked to the current resurgence of road biking, the success of Team Sky in professional road racing and the rise of the MAMIL (Middle Aged Man In Lycra). When the Financial Times says cycling "is the new golf", you'd better believe it.

Cyclosportives have their origins on the continent, especially in France and Italy. France's premier sportive is the Étape du Tour, an event where around 8,000 amateurs get to ride the 'queen stage' of that year's Tour de France race. Almost non-existent a decade ago, British sportives are growing fast, both in the number of events and their size. Many British sportives are frankly overpriced and underwhelming. Most events are on open roads and for an entry fee of as much as £50 riders get little more than a timing chip, signposts on the route, some short-dated energy bars and a cheap metal medal. You can get much better value by riding an audax event. However, there are some good sportives out there and the best are either the small, friendly, homespun events that tend to be organised by local cycling clubs or the really big, glitzy affairs run professionally that take place on roads closed to motor traffic. These big events attract tens of thousands of participants, and Velothon Wales falls firmly in the latter category.

Organised by a company that runs a similar event in Berlin, two things make the Velothon Wales special: first, it takes place on closed roads, and second, the mass participation event is followed by an elite professional race on the same route later in the day. This means there's a chance to see some of the world's top riders in action. The sportive has two distance options: 140km or 50km. The full distance route is challenging, not just because of the distance; there are some serious hill climbs, the biggest of which is the Tumble near Abergavenny. Along the way the ride takes in some great scenery in the Usk valley, the Black Mountains, the South Wales valleys and Caerphilly Mountain.

The event is bankrolled by the Welsh Government, which has allocated £900,000 for the event, spread over five years. This means it looks likely to be a permanent midsummer fixture in Wales's cycling calendar, at least until 2019. Much of that cash will be spent on the road closures that are essential for a professional bike race. As an amateur rider, having the roads to yourself is a rare privilege. It's no wonder the 15,000 places are filled within days.

Start/Finish: Cardiff
£55 for the full distance route,
£40 for the shorter route.
www.velothon-wales.co.uk/

Rhosili beach

GOWER CYCLING FESTIVAL

A week of guided rides and fun events in South Wales's
stunning Gower peninsula

In 1956 the Gower peninsula was the first part of the UK to be declared an Area of Outstanding Natural Beauty. Too small and not wild enough to be a national park, an AONB was the next best thing. And in the half century since, the many glories of the Gower – its beaches and its castles, its moorlands and megalithic monuments, its heaths and marshes, its fields and forests – have been discovered by lovers of the wild. Yet the daily commuter traffic to and from Swansea and the flood of tourists each summer means the Gower's roads can be busy, especially on the south coast where all the best beaches are. That's why I made the hard decision not to include a Gower route in the book. But help is at hand in the form of the annual Gower Cycling Festival run by Wheelrights, the Swansea Bay cycle campaign group.

This is a week-long festival in early August, including more than 20 rides of varied distance and terrain, from short, traffic-free family rides to longer, full-day rides around the Gower and much further afield, north of Swansea to Carreg Cennen Castle and to the mountain-biking mecca of the Afan Valley.

"We were inspired by the Gower Walking Festival," explains festival co-ordinator David Naylor. "We provide a menu to suit all abilities from families with small children to quite challenging rides. We've attracted people from across the country and even overseas and we're now trying to encourage more people to come and make a week of it. We've got our own festival campsite at Dunvant in the Clyne Valley. This is where most of the rides start from."

As well as the campsite there are plenty of holiday cottage, hotel and B&B options on the Gower, which is well set up for tourism, with plenty of pubs, cafés and tea rooms en route. And yet there are still several spectacular, completely unspoiled beaches like Three Cliffs Bay as well as wild rocky coastline like Worm's Head at the western end of the peninsula.

All the rides are led by experienced local cyclists. Riding in a group with a leader and a back-marker means there's some safety in numbers for the few short, unavoidable sections of main road. Typically there are about a dozen riders on each ride, though as many as 30 on the most popular. As well as knowing the best routes and the best places to stop for refreshments, many of the ride leaders are well-versed in the history and culture of the area.

Among the highlights is the Grand Gower Circuit, which takes in a stunning but perfectly rideable off-road section from Rhossili to Hillend and an optional spin across the beach at Broughton Bay. "When the tide's out, the sand is firm enough to cycle on," says David, the festival co-ordinator. There's a ride around some of the haunts of the poet Dylan Thomas and an evening ride for folk music and song at the Loughor Boat Club.

£5 registration fee
20+ rides, from 6 to 96 km (4 to 60 miles)
www.gowercyclingfestival.org

BIG APPLE BIKE RIDE

Good company on a relaxed, turn-up-and-ride spin through
the cider orchards of Herefordshire

———

Herefordshire is cider country and, twice a year for the past two decades, the village of Much Marcle holds its Big Apple weekend. It's the perfect time to visit the area, as orchards, cider mills, country houses, churches and villages halls all throw open their doors to anyone with a taste for cider and its under-appreciated cousin, perry, made in a similar way, but from pears. There are cider-making demonstrations, exhibitions of rare varieties of apples and pears, cider teas, church bell-ringing workshops and plenty of tastings of fruit, juice and intoxicating liquor. On the Sunday in the October edition that's known as 'Harvestime', local resident Bella Johnson leads a Big Apple Bike Ride from Ledbury, a handsome market town that's done a lot to welcome cyclists to the area. The destination is Much Marcle, and the ride calls in on various festival sites along the route.

"We're very welcoming and I really try to make a point of engaging people with their surroundings," Bella explains, "so we stop for a breather at places where there's some local folklore to talk about, or where a local farmer is raising some interesting breeds. There's lot of local knowledge along the way. It's 16 miles with only one steep hill, otherwise it's very manageable. Last year we had a granny and her eight-year-old grandson who absolutely loved it."

The ride is free to join and starts at the Market House in Ledbury. There are hire bikes available from Ledbury Cycle Hire, almost next door to the railway station. The route follows quiet lanes beside orchards where trees groan under the weight of the apples and pears still awaiting harvest. Besides all the cider fun, it's worth having a look around Much Marcle itself, as it's an interesting village. Stop in at the church of St Bartholomew to see its collection of beautifully carved tombs, including an effigy of Blanche Mortimer, of the bloodthirsty family of Marcher lords, described by Simon Jenkins as "Much Marcle's sleeping beauty". Look out too for the church's six green men, also carved in stone. Nearby is Hellens, the big, historic house of the village which, while very tastefully conserved and full of antique furniture, fabric and works of art, is much more of a real home than a stuffy museum.

The ride attracts a crowd of around 30 to 50 cyclists, a mixture of locals and visitors. "The whole area is incredibly friendly," says Bella. "People who come along are just wowed by the hospitality and the good cheer, as well as the cider. And apart from the one year when I was away and my husband led it, we've always had good weather!"

Start/finish: Ledbury.
26 km / 16 miles, easy going country lanes.
Free, just turn up and ride
www.bigapple.org.uk/
www.comecyclingledbury.com/

ELGAR VINTAGE RIDE

A stylish spin around the Malvern Hills in the tyre tracks
of England's favourite composer

One of the great cycling sequences in the history of film is in Ken Russell's 1962 feature-documentary about the English composer Edward Elgar. It's shot in black and white and depicts the struggling composer, still on the verge of making it big, out on his bike in the Malvern Hills. As Elgar rides, his luxuriously textured orchestral music swirls around in his head. He climbs through fields and forests, and the music builds, reaching a crescendo when he crests the summit high above the patchwork landscape of England, he and his bike silhouetted by dazzling sunbeams (you can see the clip on YouTube.) It's a fabulous piece of film-making and all the better for being based on a true story. Living in Malvern, Elgar took up cycling in 1900 at the age of 43 and named his bicycle, a black-enamelled fixed wheel model by Royal Sunbeam, 'Mr Phoebus'. The pair spent many happy days exploring the lanes around Malvern and, later, Hereford. "My idea is that there is music in the air, music all around me", he once said. "I do all my composing in the open. At home all I have to do is write it down."

It's therefore fitting that every September, cyclists from Malvern and further afield meet for an Elgar-themed ride to celebrate the town's most famous cyclist. As a founding member of the Tweed Cycling Club I take my share of the blame for the retro cycling movement that's swept the globe over the past decade. Vintage bike events and tweed rides have sprung up across Britain, France, the United States, Australia and Japan as people look to have fun while recapturing the spirit and the style of the golden era of cycling, whether that's the 1890s, the 1930s or the 1950s.

The event is organised by Nick and Tanya Trotman, who run Malvern Cycles in a building that's been a cycle shop since the 1940s. The route is 44 miles long and calls in at plenty of places with an Elgar association, with stops for refreshments at pubs along the route and at the Elgar Birthplace Museum near Worcester. The £20 entry fee includes basic refreshments and a commemorative bottle of local wine from the Frome Valley Vineyard. For anyone not up to the full distance, the ride begins with a 5-6 mile loop of Malvern, which Tanya describes as "more of a parade". This is a ride for vintage bikes and riders in period costume, though it's by no means strictly Edwardian; anything from the 1970s or earlier is welcome. Previous editions have included all kinds of pedal-powered contraptions, from penny farthings to classic roadsters to 1960s Moultons and even a Sinclair C5 pedal-car.

Start/finish: Malvern

70km / 44 miles on B-roads and country lanes, some hilly

Entry fee £20

www.elgarvintageride.co.uk

Lost Lanes
36 Glorious Bike Rides in
Wales and the Borders

Words and photos:
Jack Thurston

Cover illustrations:
Andrew Pavitt

Design and layout:
Amy Bolt
Marcus Freeman
Oliver Mann

Editorial:
Siobhan Kelly
Michael Lee

Proofreading:
Michael Lee
Candida Frith-Macdonald

Distributed by:
Central Books Ltd
99 Wallis Road
London, E9 5LN
Tel +44 (0)845 458 9911
orders@centralbooks.com

Mapping powered by:

Published by:
Wild Things Publishing Ltd
Freshford, Bath, BA2 7WG

www.wildthingspublishing.com
lostlanes.thebikeshow.net

Copyright

First edition published in the United Kingdom in 2015 by
Wild Things Publishing Ltd, Bath, United Kingdom.

Copyright © 2015 Jack Thurston.

A catalogue record of this book is available from the British Library.
ISBN-13: 978-1910636039

Photographs and maps

Acknowledgements

I'm grateful to the friends and family who've joined me on the rides, modelled for photographs, offered advice and helped check routes. Thanks to Megan de Silva and Tim Carter, Hannah Boyton, Heulwen, James and Oscar Hudson, Sam, Chloe, Oliver and Elise Charrington, Fraser Stephens, Dan Fairbank, Daniel Start, Tania Pascoe and Rose Start, Ed Wright, Julian Sayarer, Jet McDonald, Jed Price, David Price, Peter Charles-Jones, Gwenda Owen, Graham Lewis, Paul Jones, Stephen Taylor, Chester & North Wales CTC, Abergavenny Cycle Group, Owen Davies, Tanya Trotman, Bella Johnson, Ed Robson, Alistair Baglee, David Naylor, George Burgess and Lisa Roberts. Special thanks to Matthew Walters for being the perfect cycle touring companion.

Many thanks to Andrew for another cracking cover illustration and to Amy Bolt for the superb design work, especially the new maps, for which thanks also to Richard Fairhurst at cycle.travel. Thanks to Siobhan and Michael for adding some polish to the text and to Candida for the eagle eyes. The responsibility for any mistakes and wrong turns is all mine. Huge thanks to Daniel for all the encouragement, gentle whip-cracking and many years of bike adventures. Greatest thanks of all to Sarah and Lewin for sharing a passion for exploring our beautiful country on two wheels.

Ride 17 is dedicated to the memory of Jeremy Price, who loved those hills.